THE GREAT MASTERS OF DRAWING

DRAWINGS BY
MICHELANGELO

BY

MARIA VITTORIA BRUGNOLI

TRANSLATED BY

HELEN AND DAVID FRIEDMAN

DOVER PUBLICATIONS, INC., NEW YORK

Published in Canada by
GENERAL PUBLISHING COMPANY, LTD.,
30 LESMILL ROAD, DON MILLS, TORONTO, ONTARIO

Published in the United Kingdom by
CONSTABLE AND COMPANY, LTD.,
10 ORANGE STREET, LONDON WC2.

Drawings by Michelangelo is a new translation, first published by Dover
Publications, Inc., in 1969, of the work originally published by Aldo
Martello, Milan, 1964, in his series "I Grandi Maestri del Disegno." The
present edition, which contains all the original illustrations and adds a List
of Plates, is published by special arrangement with Mr. Martello.

Standard Book Number: 486-21991-7
Library of Congress Catalog Card Number: 67-28635
Manufactured in the United States of America

DOVER PUBLICATIONS, INC.
180 VARICK STREET, NEW YORK, N.Y. 10014

MICHELANGELO'S FIGURE DRAWINGS

EVEN a brief discussion, such as ours must be, of the drawings of Michelangelo is a task whose difficulties must necessarily be emphasized: difficulties created by the extremely high quality of the drawings—among the greatest of all time—and by the unusually varied and complex problems, still in part unsolved, that they present. We will limit our discussion to the figure drawings, purposely setting aside the architectural drawings, which are important enough to demand an independent treatment.

Bernard Berenson showed that he had studied the subject thoroughly and successfully when, in the introduction to his 1903 catalogue of Michelangelo figure drawings—the first systematic, and still fundamental, catalogue of the material—he warned about the particularly difficult problems of dating and attribution which those drawings presented in addition to the standard problems of examining and judging any drawing. Berenson's views have been acknowledged and confirmed in the last six decades in many, sometimes excellent, articles. Different, often sharply conflicting, opinions have been advanced and convincingly argued concerning a large number of the drawings.

There has been a growing tendency to replace the "restrictive" criterion of attribution championed by Morelli—who assigned an excessively limited number of sheets to Michelangelo—by the recognition of Michelangelo's hand in many drawings which had previously been dismissed as copies or had been attributed to more or less accomplished artists who worked in the circle of the master. As a result of this trend many scholars have come to claim as works of Michelangelo the generous group of drawings catalogued by Berenson under the rubric Sebastiano del Piombo. In some cases, as for example the Uffizi drawing for *The Battle of Cascina* (Plate 12) or *The Archers* (Plate 44), to limit ourselves to a few examples reproduced here, a new authoritative assertion has been made that they are completely by Michelangelo. In other cases, as for example *The Dream* (Plate 45), discussion is still open.

One should not be misled by the great differences of opinion concerning the quality and the chronology of the drawings into thinking that the personality of the artist, which is so powerfully and decisively manifested elsewhere, expresses itself inadequately or somewhat elusively in the graphic medium. One must rather keep in mind, besides the general problems indicated by Berenson, the fact that only a few of the surviving drawings by Michelangelo relate closely to projects completed by him in sculpture or painting. At the same time, the great fame which the artist came to enjoy as early as the period of the decoration of the Sistine ceiling made his drawings highly sought after. This, in turn, generated a spate of imitations and copies, which were often done by expert, and sometimes by contemporary, hands.

Moreover, a study of the peculiarities of Michelangelo's drawing style is of little help in attempting to establish a chronology. The style varied only little in the long years preceding 1530 and was characterized by recurring traits. A study of the types of figures, of their movements and of the composition of the groups is also of limited use. Michelangelo frequently took up a theme he had treated many years before, and thus his drawings often have no direct connection with the large works he was currently occupied with. The drawings are primarily concerned with a constant search for expression urged by his own intimate thoughts and by his extreme and unreserved sensitivity to the tormenting problem of human existence.

Michelangelo was by nature a sculptor and always desirous of producing a powerful effect of plasticity and tension. The graphic media, whether pen, black crayon or red crayon, provided him with an ideal tool for the translation into visual terms of his great dream of an heroic humanity animated by the profound knowledge of its own spiritual values and determined to defend them to the last breath, without overemphasizing the great physical size of the figures which was merely the instrument and the image of that great and noble fight.

The same vigorous strokes which, from the very earliest drawings, determine the contours of the figure create the figure's ample plasticity, and subject the natural element to an ideal form conceived in terms of a superhuman grandeur that transcends any reality. These same strokes become more numerous and more closely spaced, overlapping and crossing, when the energy of the modeling is to be emphasized. The shadows become dense in order to throw the contrasting light areas into the most forceful relief. This is drawing "from dark to light," as Panofsky rightly characterized it. In this opposition of light and darkness we can see the tense dialectic between energy and inert mass, between spiritual and material elements, which remains a constant feature of the art of Michelangelo, occupying every fiber of the artist throughout his entire life until the very dramatic resolution of this tension in his latest work.

Drawings like those in Plates 3 through 8, dating from the very first years of the sixteenth century, attain an expressiveness in no way inferior to Michelangelo's contemporary achievements in other media, such as the *David*, *The Madonna of Bruges*, the Pitti *tondo* (roundel) and the Doni *tondo*. And a comparison of the drawings with the artist's production with chisel or brush in the succeeding decades leads to the same conclusion. In fact, the violence of a gesture or a movement is often freed by the black stroke of a pen or crayon on the white paper with an impulsiveness that translates into a visual image the first formulation of a concept, introducing us—and this cannot happen without turbulence—to the very heart of the initial act of creation.

I am thinking of drawings, like those in Plates 9, 12, 40 and 57, that most explicitly present the character of sketches and consequently the character of a direct translation of an idea. Because this idea is transformed and varied in the very act of emerging, it reveals the riot of images which crowd the artist's mind. This great freedom and fertility of imagination was characteristic of Michelangelo; he applied himself indefatigably to the theme of man and his existence, proposing ever new solutions, which reveal, in every gesture and in every movement, the unqualified commitment of the artist.

Because of all this it can be supposed that Michelangelo's drawings, even had they come down to us in greater number, rarely would have permitted precise comparisons with his works of sculpture or painting. They were done for their own sake and are fundamental, rather than complementary, to the study of his art. That the artist himself thought of the drawings in this way is indicated by the fact that in them he planned compositions, even bringing them to a high state of finish, whose reappearance in either the completed works of the artist, or in ones which he might have projected but never executed, is very hypothetical. This is the case with the "divine heads" that Michelangelo gave to Gherardo Perini (Plate 27), the drawings for Cavalieri (Plates 42 and 43), the drawing for a *Resurrection* (Plates 37 and 38) and the drawing for a *Sacrifice of Isaac* (Plate 41). All of this cannot but increase our great regret for the cruel loss of much of the graphic production of the artist; a loss caused in part by the desire of the artist himself, who burned his cartoons and drawings, and not only in the last days of his life (as we learn from Vasari and from some letters of Aretino written in 1538 and 1546), but to a much greater extent by the negligence of the men to whom the drawings were entrusted and, ultimately, by the confusion of the times.

The sheets, of almost uniformly high quality, which have been preserved allow us to examine in its successive phases the ceaseless creative process which occupied Michelangelo for his entire lifetime.

The earliest drawings that have come down to us are studies after Giotto, Masaccio and ancient statues. These are more than experiments. In each of them Michelangelo establishes the essential of the representation of a human figure of great physical power and extreme nobility of spirit. There is a great energy in the stroke which articulates the heavy folds of drapery and the solid musculature. Already he shows a sure understanding of the usefulness of *contrapposto* for the expression of the vitality of the masses. All the tension of these is concentrated in the expressions of the faces. These are individuals determined to attain full consciousness of themselves and of their own significance as men, as created beings.

This noble aspiration presupposes the great experience of the Renaissance, but pushed to the breaking point. The drawing in Plate 4, dated about the time of the *David* of the Piazza della Signoria—and not only because of the similarity of the pose of the heroic nude Mercury —already shows the break. The equilibrium within which the inflated musculature is confined is about to be disrupted. The internal tension will soon be transported to the surface, upset the balance and substitute for this balance a conflict of forces which it will be impossible to resolve.

The theme of movement, increasingly understood as the irreconcilable conflict between spirit and matter, will occupy the mind of the artist completely from now on. This contrast is individuated in every figure and is only resolved when the individual is set alone, as if outside of himself, to confront the dilemma. Because of this isolation, the gesture, rather than unfolding itself in time or space, is jammed in a state of potential movement, as if it were confined by force within the volume of a block of marble. This is a method of facing and resolving the problem which derives from the sculptural practice of the artist. For him the barely roughhewn block of stone already contained all the elements necessary to define the image. The act of bringing the image to light assumed a value of its own that was more moral than it was artistic.

In the early years of the sixteenth century, when work was begun on the tremendous project for the cartoon of *The Battle of Cascina*, Michelangelo came into close contact with Leonardo da Vinci (it was Leonardo's second Florentine period). It is at least possible that the relationship between them was of some importance for the introduction of the problem of motion in the mind of the younger artist. Drawings such as those for a *St. Anne* (Plate 5) or a cavalry battle (Plate 9) seem to provide indisputable proof of this. It is, however, necessary to note at once that the conclusions at which the two artists arrive, if not actually antithetical, are very different. Leonardo resolves the movement-generating conflict of energy and mass in a cosmic equilibrium based on the supreme Reason which governs the world. Because of the capacity of the human mind to understand the laws which regulate the natural world, man finds his own equilibrium and his own reason for existence. This is fundamentally a "classical" and Renaissance conception because of its complete faith in man's ability and belief in his oneness with the universe. Man participates in the vital energy, the spiritual force which pervades the world. To understand the *causes* of this force is to impose a logical control on it which excludes every primitive fear and, at the same time, recognizes the necessary and positive value of *mass*, that is, the inanimate matter which is the antithesis of that force.

If the element of force in this dialectic were to escape the close control of Reason, the other element, mass, would once more assume its full character of brutal inertia, the negation of the concept of spiritual energy. The fight between the two would then become strenuous and debilitating, and the possibility of reconciliation would no longer exist. This is what takes place in the work of Michelangelo, who accepts the burden of the crisis of the Renaissance world, recognizing its terms in the Neoplatonic doctrine in which the Christian concept of the absolute transcendence of the divine is revived. The opposition of the active form of the spirit, an eternal element of divine substance, to the immobility of matter is understood by the new ethic consciousness of Neoplatonism as the irreconcilable conflict between Good and Evil—the eternal dualism inherent in human nature. Once more this dualism suggests itself to man with dramatic violence, imposing a denial of all faith in the "natural" possibilities of the individual, in a final hope of salvation.

This is a definite change from the rational balance of the Renaissance and we can only expect a corresponding change within the expressive means. The exquisite painterly luminosity which pervades the atmosphere of Leonardo's pictures and envelops all the figures in it is replaced by a sharp contrast of light and shade which becomes increasingly relentless. Light does not merely articulate the surface from the outside by throwing the recessed parts into shadow, but itself carves the form. It is an expression of that energy which, "*per forza di levare*" (Michelangelo's famous description of the process of sculpturing in marble, as opposed to modeling in clay, which literally means "by the process of taking away"), frees form from the indistinct darkness of the material in which it is enclosed. As Panofsky noted, it would not be correct on that account to speak of the "painterliness" of Michelangelo. Neither is this justified by his *figura serpentinata*, attractive to Michelangelo because it is a most effective means for expressing, through the counterpoises along the curved axis, the conflict of forces which sustain and animate the figure, rather than creating an imaginary extension into surrounding space such as Leonardo's "spiral" did. Michelangelo himself is said to have described the *figura serpentinata* to his pupil Marco Pino as a figure "multiplied by one, two and three" and "the figure of a tongue of fire." Michelangelo began to utilize the *figura serpentinata* as he became increasingly aware of the drama of the human condition during the last years of the decoration of the ceiling of the Sistine Chapel.

At this stage one may certainly speak of an increased subtlety of color and chiaroscuro in Michelangelo's work. Thus, in the drawings for the Prophet Jonah (Plate 23) and for the Libyan Sibyl (Plate 24) the diffused line of the red crayon brings an unprecedented anxiety to the clairvoyance of the Prophet and to the twisted limbs of the Sibyl, the last of the *ignudi*, which reaffirms the ethical value of physical beauty. Michelangelo's form is continually being enriched by new modulations and at the same time proclaims unimpaired faith in a significance of form that goes beyond a vigorous definition of physique. This is an ideal form in which the mind and the eye of the artist, never dominated by the particular data of nature, search for a reflection of supreme Beauty and at the same time seek a way, the only way, of ascending to it.

Gli occhi miei vaghi delle cose belle	Beautiful things are the longing of my eyes,
e l'alma insieme della sua salute	Just as it is my soul's to be secure,
non hanno altra virtute	But they've no other power
c'ascenda al ciel, che mirar tutte quelle.	That lifts to Heaven, but staring at all those.*
[FREY EDITION, CIX, 99]	

One can hardly be astonished, then, that a young athlete supplies the torso of the Libyan Sibyl in the Metropolitan Museum drawing, or that the head of Jonah is similar enough to the head of the Virgin of the Doni *tondo* to have been considered a study for it.

* Translation by Creighton Gilbert, in *Complete Poems and Selected Letters of Michelangelo*, Random House, New York, 1963, pp. 76–77.

The exaltation of the human being, which sustains the Prophets and Sibyls of the Sistine Chapel, animates the faultless harmony of the nude Adam and Eve in the *Creation* and *Sin* episodes and stimulates the tension of the young *ignudi*, could not be repeated in the later works of Michelangelo.

Some of this exaltation is preserved in the extremely fine *Captives* for the tomb of Julius II, now in the Louvre (*cf.* Plate 25), but even here there is a different understanding of the human condition and a definite indication of the direction in which Michelangelo's style will turn in the statues for the Medici Chapel. The unending confrontation with the external world and with his own fate produces an increasing harshness and irritability in the artist and the man. His faith in the possibilities of the individual vacillates. The extreme sadness and hopelessness of the *Night* and the *Evening* seem to express this. The two nude figures are barely rounded out compared with the imposing plasticity of the nudes in the Sistine Chapel. The constriction of the giant figure of *Day* and the power of its swollen masses within the grip of the marble block is an explicit repudiation of this faith.

We now see in Michelangelo's sculpture the increasing prevalence of his *non finito* (an expression which has stimulated many subtle critical interpretations). The material itself assumes an increasingly greater importance. Parts of the stone are left only roughly blocked out. The marks of the claw chisel are retained (see the Medici *Madonna* and the Accademia *Captives*). The areas of light are limited, accenting the tense potentiality of motion in the figure to the point of making it spasmodic.

In the drawings, the increasing importance of the areas of shadow (*cf.* Plates 33 and 36) seems to have the same significance. This results in an intensified concentration of the figure as it assumes full consciousness in the deepest part of its own being (*cf.* Plates 27 and 35) of an ineluctable reality, the sorrowful destiny of the human race. The elements of the Michelangelesque dialogue are completely polarized, but they have still not reached the extent of opposition which would destroy the possibility of their coexistence.

The brief period of renewed classic equilibrium, almost a yearning for the recovery of the irretrievable ideals of his youth, which marks Michelangelo's first encounter with his friend Tommaso Cavalieri (*cf.* Plates 42–44) will shortly give way—perhaps under the influence of Vittoria Colonna's austere religiosity, expressed in ardent terms of sin and salvation—to the supreme human tragedy of the Sistine *Last Judgment*. But that itself is an expression, the last, of an heroic humanity which, even when confronted with a hopeless fight, by the very act of facing the desperate conflict reaffirms the nobility of its whole being, both mind and body. The long human and artistic struggle has not extinguished in Michelangelo the Renaissance man, who is present with every fiber in the titanic will which propels the groups of the damned toward the unattainable height of Christ the Judge.

That these damned are the characters in the drama who were closest in spirit to the artist, himself torn by the same conflict, and, as such, those who chiefly stimulated his inexhaustible creativity, is shown by the drawings for *The Last Judgment* (Plates 48 and 49), in which the theme of the outcasts is set forth with insistence, resolving itself in a succession of lines of force which enclose the abnormally muscular masses of the nudes and constrict the figures into a tight body, thereby creating an image of the inexorable meshes of the fate which draws them together.

In the large, but less articulated, bodies of the figures in the frescoes of the Pauline Chapel we no longer recognize the imposing vitality of the figures of *The Last Judgment*. The aggressive engagement of the figures of the Sistine Chapel fresco with the viewer is replaced in the Pauline frescoes by an appeal to him that is full of pathos. Times and spirits have changed. The Counter-Reformation is in the air, and already we sense its rigid dogmatism. There is no hope for man except with the aid of Grace. In a new flight into mysticism, craving for salvation replaces the pride of individual assertion.

The overwhelming presence of mass in the Pauline frescoes is itself a condemnation of man's mortal state because more strongly and explicitly than ever before, it declares the body to be an earthly prison in whose cruel confines the human soul recognizes itself ineluctably constrained.

Michelangelo nevertheless wanted to answer with a last message of hope the desperate question posed in the contorted glances of the women who stare at the spectator from the sides of *The Crucifixion of St. Peter*: in the marble *Pietàs* of the last years and in the drawings of *The Crucifixion* (Plates 58 and 59) he wanted to show to mankind, and to himself, the last and, for his battleweary spirit, only way by which man may absolve himself of the compulsion with which he was burdened by his origin. The progressive corruption of physical substance signals the rejection of the last ideals of the Renaissance. But the final act of the ninety-year-old artist is once more an act of faith and love. In the anxious gesture of the Mother who presses her young Son to her (see Plate 60) he confirms an unshaken faith in the highest capacity of the human spirit.

A NOTE ON THE COLLECTIONS

THE largest present-day collections of Michelangelo drawings had their origin chiefly in the complex of drawings, sketches and studies which were to be found at the death of the artist in the house of his family on Via Ghibellina and in the *bottega* on Via Mozza in Florence.

The drawings which were found in the workshop were given to the Grand Duke Cosimo de' Medici by Lionardo Buonarroti. From the Medici collection they later entered the Gabinetto dei Disegni of the Uffizi. Some of these drawings were returned by the Medici to the Buonarroti heirs in the first decades of the seventeenth century, when the house on Via Ghibellina was made into a museum. The collection of the Casa Buonarroti thus became the most important collection of Michelangelo drawings and has remained so to this day despite the severe diminution it suffered in the nineteenth century at the hands of the descendants of the artist.

The drawings sold by the Buonarroti heirs traveled to England, where they formed the nucleus of the Michelangelo collections of the British Museum and the Ashmolean Museum, the two most important collections after those of the Casa Buonarroti and the Uffizi.

On the other hand, many of the Michelangelo drawings of the Royal Collection at Windsor Castle have a Roman, rather than a Florentine, provenance. Among these are the drawings given by Michelangelo to Tommaso Cavalieri, which belonged, at the end of the sixteenth century, to Cardinal Alessandro Farnese.

The drawings of the Teyler Museum in Haarlem also come from Rome. Acquired in the eighteenth century from the Odescalchi family, they seem to have belonged to Queen Christine of Sweden in the seventeenth century.

The collection of Michelangelo drawings in the Louvre originated in the collection of the King of France, in which, as early as the beginning of the eighteenth century, were gathered a sizable number of drawings by the artist. This collection, like the English ones, was increased through the nineteenth century by purchases and donations.

The collection of the Albertina in Vienna is composed of drawings which once belonged to the great eighteenth-century French collector Mariette. They were bought after the Frenchman's collection had been dispersed following his death in 1774.

Only a few drawings are now owned by public or private collectors other than those mentioned above. It should, however, be pointed out that some of these drawings, as for example the *Five Studies* in the Chantilly Museum and the *Study for the Libyan Sibyl* in the Metropolitan Museum of New York, are of very high quality.

For information concerning collections of Michelangelo drawings see the introductions to the catalogues of the individual collections cited in the Bibliographical Note. See further: A. E. Popham, *Catalogue of an Exhibition of Drawings by Michelangelo*, London, 1953; and L. Dussler, *Die Zeichnungen des Michelangelo*, Berlin, 1959.

ACKNOWLEDGMENTS

It gives me great pleasure to acknowledge the prompt assistance I have received from colleagues in museums throughout the world in the collection of reproductions of drawings in the possession of their institutions, and to thank them for giving their permission to publish them. Particular thanks are due to Prof. Giulia Sinibaldi, Director of the Gabinetto dei Disegni of the Uffizi; Mr. Philip Pouncey, of the Department of Drawings of the British Museum; Mr. K. T. Parker, Director of the Ashmolean Museum; Miss Scott Elliot of the Royal Library of Windsor Castle; Mme. Bouchot Saupique and Mlle. Roseline Bacou of the Cabinet des Dessins of the Louvre; Mr. Jacob Bean of the Department of Drawings of the Metropolitan Museum of New York; and finally Count Antoine Seilern, who generously permitted the reproduction of the drawing in his collection.

BIBLIOGRAPHICAL NOTE

Owing to the vastness of the Michelangelo bibliography, including works relative to the drawings, we must limit ourselves here to an indication of the general bibliographies (through 1961) and a list, alphabetized by author, of the catalogues of the larger collections of Michelangelo drawings and of the publications cited in the text.

STEINMANN, E., & R. WITTKOWER
Michelangelo Bibliographie 1510–1926, Leipzig, 1927.

SCHMIDT, H. W.
"Nachtrag und Fortsetzung der Michelangelo Bibliographie von Steinmann-Wittkower bis 1930," appendix to E. Steinmann, *Michelangelo im Spiegel seiner Zeit*, Leipzig, 1930.

CHERUBELLI, P.
"Supplemento alla bibliografia michelangiolesca (1931–1942)," *Centenario del Giudizio*, 1942.

BAROCCHI, P.
"Bibliografia michelangiolesca dal 1942 al 1961," in G. Vasari, *La Vita di Michelangelo*, Milan-Naples, 1962, Vol. I, pp. 339 ff.

Among the most recent additions to the literature on Michelangelo's drawings we would like to point out the article by M. Hirst, "Michelangelo Drawings in Florence," *Burlington Magazine*, April 1963, pp. 166 ff.

ARETINO, P.
Lettere, ed. E. Camesasca, 1957.

BAROCCHI, P.
Michelangelo e la sua scuola; i disegni di Casa Buonarroti e degli Uffizi, Florence, 1962.

BERENSON, B.
The Drawings of the Florentine Painters, London, 1903; 2nd ed., Chicago, 1938.

BRUGNOLI, M. V.
"Note sul rapporto Leonardo-Michelangelo," *Bollettino d'Arte*, 1955, pp. 124 ff.

CELLINI, B.
Vita, Florence, critical ed. of 1901.

CONDIVI, A.
Vita di Michelangelo, Rome, 1553.

DEMONTS, L.
Musée du Louvre—Les Dessins de Michel-Ange, Paris, 1921.

FREY, C.
Die Dichtungen des Michelagniolo, Berlin, 1897.

LOMAZZO, G. P.
Trattato dell'Arte della Pittura, Milan, 1584.

MARABOTTINI, A.
"Il 'Sogno' di Michelangelo," in *Scritti . . . in onore di L. Venturi*, 1956, pp. 349 ff.

MORELLI, G.
"Handzeichnungen italienischer Meister," *Kunstchronik*, Neue Folge III, 1891–92, pp. 290 ff.; IV, 1892–93, pp. 54 ff.

PANOFSKY, E.
Die Handzeichnungen Michelangelos, Leipzig, 1922.

PANOFSKY, E.
Studies in Iconology, 2nd ed., New York, 1962.

PARKER, K. T.
Catalogue of the Drawings in the Ashmolean Museum, II, Oxford, 1956.

POPHAM-WILDE,
The Italian Drawings of the XV–XVI Centuries . . . at Windsor Castle, London, 1949

POPP, A. E.
Die Medici-Kapelle, Munich, 1922.

STIX, A., & L. FRÖHLICH BUME
Die Zeichnungen der toskanischen, umbrischen und römischen Schulen (Beschreibender Katalog der Handzeichnungen in der . . . Albertina, III), Vienna, 1932.

TOLNAY, C.
Michelangelo, 5 vols., Princeton, 1943–60.

VASARI, G.
La Vita di Michelangelo, edited and with a commentary by P. Barocchi, 5 vols., Milan-Naples, 1962.

WILDE, J.
Italian Drawings . . . in the British Museum—Michelangelo and his Studio, London, 1953.

WITTKOWER, R.
"Physiognomical Experiments by Michelangelo . . .," *Journal of the Warburg Institute*, I, 1937–38, pp. 183 ff.

LIST OF PLATES

1 Figure study after Giotto's *Apotheosis of St. John the Baptist*
2 Figure study after Masaccio's *Sagra of the Carmine*
3 Five studies
4 Study for a *Mercury* (?)
5 Madonna and Child with St. Anne
6 Sketch for a bronze *David*
7 Studies of cherubs
8 Various studies
9 Study for *The Battle of Cascina*: Cavalry battle
10 Study for *The Battle of Cascina*: Young male nude
11 Study for *The Battle of Cascina*: Studies of figures and *The Madonna of Bruges*
12 Study for *The Battle of Cascina*: Studies of figures
13 Study for *The Battle of Cascina*: Nude
14 Study for *The Battle of Cascina*: Nude
15 Study for *The Battle of Cascina*: Skirmish between cavalry and foot soldiers
16 Study of a nude
17 Madonna and Child with St. Anne
18 Study for the Sistine ceiling: Architectural project with Apostles
19 Study for the Sistine ceiling: Adam in *The Expulsion from Paradise*
20 Study for the Sistine ceiling: Head of an old man
21 Study for the Sistine ceiling: Head of a young man
22 Study for the Sistine ceiling: Nude
23 Study for the Sistine ceiling: Head
24 Study for the Sistine ceiling: The Libyan Sibyl
25 Study for the Sistine ceiling: *Genietto*
26 Study for a Prophet (?)
27 Study of a female head
28 Study for the Medici Chapel: River god
29 Study for the Medici Chapel: Anatomical study
30 Study for the Medici Chapel: Grotesque heads
31 Study for the Medici Chapel: Monstrous animal
32 Study for a *Madonna and Child*
33 Study for a *Holy Family*
34 Head of a young man
35 Head of a young woman
36 Study for an *Adoration of the Bronze Serpent*
37 Study for a *Resurrection*
38 Study for a *Resurrection*
39 Study for a *Resurrected Christ*
40 Figure study
41 Sacrifice of Isaac
42 Tityus
43 Fall of Phaëthon
44 The Archers
45 The Dream
46 Study of a head
47 Study for *The Last Judgment*: Compositional study
48 Study for *The Last Judgment*: Compositional study
49 Study for *The Last Judgment*: Compositional study
50 Study for *The Last Judgment*: The Deacon Lawrence
51 Study for *The Last Judgment*: Figure study
52 Cartoon for three soldiers from *The Crucifixion of St. Peter*
53 Madonna and Child
54 Christ expels the money-changers from the Temple
55 Epiphany
56 The Virgin of the Annunciation
57 Sketches for a *Pietà*
58 The Crucifixion
59 The Crucifixion
60 Madonna and Child

DESCRIPTION OF PLATES

1 & 2. These are among the earliest known drawings by Michelangelo. They are attributed by all students to the period of the artist's apprenticeship in the workshop of Domenico and David Ghirlandaio, which he entered in 1488, when he was barely thirteen (Vasari). About a year later he entered the school in the Garden of Piazza San Marco founded by Lorenzo the Magnificent. In the first drawing Michelangelo copies two figures from Giotto's fresco *The Apotheosis of St. John the Baptist* in the Peruzzi Chapel in Santa Croce. In the second he copies a group of figures from the *Sagra* (Consecration) *of the Carmine*, the fresco, destroyed in 1600, that Masaccio painted in the cloister of the convent of the Carmine.

Domenico Ghirlandaio also used a group of figures from the *Sagra* in one of his frescoes in the Sassetti Chapel and so it has been supposed that in the Vienna drawing the young Michelangelo copied a study or a lost work by the head of the workshop. But both the exact correspondence of the three Michelangelo figures to one of the groups in the Carmine fresco (*cf.* the late sixteenth-century copy of the lost fresco in the Folkstone Museum—*Paragone*, May 1962, Fig. 54) and considerations of the style of the drawing make this hypothesis improbable.

In the very selection of his models—Giotto and Masaccio—the young artist already shows his orientation toward a robustly plastic form of ample volume which expresses both intense concentration and nobility.

The pen stroke in the outline is decisive. The thick hatching in shaded areas, juxtaposed with the most highly lighted parts, produces a strong relief.

Paris, Louvre, 706 *recto*; pen and ink, 317 × 204 mm; Alinari photo.

Vienna, Albertina, inv. 116 *recto*; pen and ink, 294 × 201 mm; photo by Albertina, Vienna.

3. Five Studies.—These studies demonstrate the intimate knowledge of antique statuary which Michelangelo garnered from study first in the Medici Garden and then in Rome during his first sojourn there in 1496–1501. This experience is clearly reflected in four of the figures. The Hellenistic models appear to be studied not purely from an archeological standpoint but, more importantly, as an expression of a figurative ideal similar to the artist's own. The robust anatomical articulation, emphasized by the decisive line with which the figures are drawn and by the contrast of dark against light, confers upon the nudes a vitality not present in the ancient models. The accented S-curve rhythm of the back view of the female nude is one of the typical features of Michelangelo nudes. The weighted torsion generates the effect of great energy held in check. Figures such as this had a large following among artists of the first decades of the sixteenth century, who found in them and developed from them an extremely elegant play of line not exploited in the originals.

Because of the effectiveness of the line in this drawing, it was judged by Berenson, and rightly so, as the most important among the early drawings left by the artist.

The cloaked figure in the center of the sheet seems still inspired by the *Sagra* of Masaccio. In this case, in view of the delicate intimacy of the small head, a study by Ghirlandaio may have been intermediary.

Chantilly, Condé Museum, No. 29; pen and ink, 263 × 287 mm; Giraudon photo.

4. Study for a Mercury (?)—Done at about the same time as the preceding drawing. The precise dating was made by Tolnay, who noted a similarity between the sketch at the bottom left of the sheet and a fountain statue in the Cesi garden in Rome. To the extent

that the ample mass of muscles studied from the live model is recomposed in terms of classical measure, both this superb young male nude—probably, because of the winged cap, a Mercury—and the Chantilly drawing reveal the well-assimilated inspiration of ancient sculpture. The dialogue between reality and ideal form will remain constant, even though the range of expression is very wide, until the Sistine *Last Judgment*.

The drawing of Mercury appears, for more than one reason, to be very close in time to the statue of *David*—the commission for the statue was given to the artist in August 1501. The *contrapposto* of the figure and the arm held straight down along the side and ending in a clenched fist are a prelude to the *David*. The stringed musical instrument supported by Mercury's left arm has led to the suggestion that the subject was an Apollo. This identification is associated with the notice of a statue (referred to by Condivi and Vasari as a Cupid) executed by Michelangelo during his stay in Rome from 1496 to 1501 for the banker and collector of antiquities, Jacopo Galli. The identification, however, remains questionable.

Paris, Louvre, 688 *recto*; pen and ink, 400 × 210 mm; Alinari photo.

5. Madonna and Child with St. Anne.—It is this drawing, together with some battle scenes (Plates 9 and 15), that most clearly testifies to the association between Michelangelo and Leonardo in the Florentine years from the return of the young Michelangelo from Rome to the time that he worked on the *Battle* in the Sala del Consiglio of the Palazzo Vecchio.

The character of the figures in the studies on the verso also indicates a date in the period 1501–1502 for the sheet. Most critics agree that the studies done by Leonardo for the *St. Anne* in the Louvre are the source for this composition by Michelangelo. A cartoon for Leonardo's painting, since lost, was seen in Florence in April 1501 by Pietro da Novellara, who wrote of it to Isabella d'Este. This cartoon and studies related to it could have been seen by Michelangelo after his return to Florence in the spring of 1501.

Undoubtedly the group of three figures composed on a diagonal, with the Child outside the center of the composition, has a relationship to Leonardo's studies. From these, also, derives the dynamic and tense *contrap-*

posto, which, in Michelangelo's drawing, expresses a new energy in mass. The pen strokes, longer and more widely separated than in the preceding drawings, summarize the modeling, emphasizing only a few areas of light along an oblique path running from left to right. The source of light seems to come from outside the composition, but the enveloping effect of Leonardo's chiaroscuro is replaced, characteristically for Michelangelo, by a harder light and a sculpturally precise definition of the figure group.

A special feature is the rapid sketching of the Madonna's left foot, which almost looks like the hoof of a horse. This is a characteristically Michelangelesque treatment, which reappears in later drawings by the master.

Oxford, Ashmolean Museum, Robinson 22 *recto*; pen and ink, 250 × 175 mm; Ashmolean Museum photo.

6. Sketch for a Bronze David.—The bronze *David* was commissioned by the Signoria of Florence in August 1502 at the request of Pierre de Rohan, Marshal of Giè, who in turn was acting for the King of France, who wanted to have a figure of David similar to the bronze statue by Donatello. The statue, a little smaller than life size, was well under way when the Marshal lost the favor of Louis XII in April 1504. In November 1508 the *David* was sent to Florimond Robertet, Louis' treasurer, in answer to his request. The statue was placed in the courtyard of the château of Bury near Blois, from where it was later removed. Since the middle of the seventeenth century its whereabouts have been unknown. The Louvre drawing, to be dated around 1502, is the most reliable source that remains for the appearance of this work by Michelangelo. The Donatellian theme given by the patron is completely reworked. Here an image of great energy is obtained through the taut angularity of the bent leg, the turn of the torso and the broad modeling. Because of the rapid and skillful strokes of the pen this is one of Michelangelo's most vivid drawings. It is extremely successful in expressing the bold self-assurance of the young hero. This image surely continues the moral heritage of the Renaissance more successfully than the contemporaneous marble *David* in the Piazza della Signoria, for which the sketch of the arm and shoulder at the right of the figure is

said to be a study. The first of the words written at the extreme right of the drawing refer to this *David*.

Paris, Louvre, 714 *recto*; pen and ink, 265 × 188 mm; Alinari photo.

7. Studies of Cherubs.—These seven studies of infantile figures (the sketch at the left in the middle of the page seems to have been by a student of the artist, according to Tolnay) are, in all probability, connected with the two marble *tondi*, one now in the Bargello and the other in London, executed for the Florentines Bartolomeo Pitti and Taddeo Taddei, respectively, and dating from the years between 1504 and 1506. It is difficult, as it is in the case of most Michelangelo drawings, to single out precise relationships with the sculptured figures. In this case the difficulty is increased by the fact that the poses are a series of variations on the theme of infancy, drawn from life, which show influences of the sculpture of both the fifteenth century and antiquity. Thus the child at the top right is endowed with an infantile grace reminiscent of Desiderio da Settignano, while the back view of the cherub at the bottom seems to repeat a Hellenistic motif (*cf.* the drawing by Heemskerck, *Römische Skizzenbücher*, Berlin, 1913, Vol. I, folio 37 *verso*, Fig. 38).

The increased naturalism of these figures could have been inspired by contact with Leonardo, which was particularly close during the period when Michelangelo was working on the cartoon for the *Battle*. This contact is also apparent in the Pitti and Taddei *tondi*. A more fluid relationship between light and dark, especially in the modeling of the two cherubs in the middle of the page, seems to confirm this theory.

The words "chosse de bruges" written twice in contemporary script on the sheet could refer to the statue of the *Madonna and Child* that was sent to the Mouscron heirs in Bruges in 1506. This does not, however, necessarily imply a relationship between these studies and that statuary group.

London, British Museum, 1887-5-2-117 *verso*; pen and ink, 375 × 230 mm; Alinari photo.

8. Various Studies.—This sheet, along with the preceding drawing, must be placed in the years in which Michelangelo, after his return to Florence, continually reworked the subject of the Madonna and Child in both sculpture and painting. The two *tondi*, the Pitti and the Taddei, already noted, the *tondo* commissioned by Agnolo Doni (in the Uffizi) and the statuary group in Bruges belong to this period. The chronology of these works, especially that of *The Madonna of Bruges*, for which the only sure document concerns the transportation of the statue to Flanders in August 1506, remains in question.

In this Berlin drawing the beautiful female head that occupies the right side of the page has suggested a connection with the Madonna of the Doni *tondo*, but the quality of intense concentration of the face offers an equally convincing analogy to *The Madonna of Bruges*. The compactly twisted Herculean limbs of the vigorous little Jesus remind one of the Child of the Doni *tondo*. At the same time the almost satyr-like shrewdness in the expression of the face seems to anticipate the young St. John in the same composition. In back of the small Jesus is a masculine figure, perhaps a St. Joseph, and at the top are studies of cherubs analogous to some of the figures in the preceding drawing. The severe profile, drawn with great care, on the left side of the sheet has been related to the statue of St. Matthew.

All of these elements indicate a date for this drawing around 1504. The artist's careful use of the pen seems to verify this. The pen marks, straight, curved, or hatched, achieve the subtlety of an engraved line. At the same time the gradation of the chiaroscuro is similar to that found in the studies for the cartoon of *The Battle of Cascina*, a technique not unlike that used, for example, in Plate 10.

The attribution of this Berlin drawing to Michelangelo is among the most disputed. Some critics, Berenson among them, praise the quality, while others maintain, but without persuasive arguments, that the work was done by one of Michelangelo's pupils or even by an artist of the fifteenth century.

Berlin, Kupferstichkabinett, No. 1363; pen and ink, 285 × 210mm; photo Berlin, Kupferstichkabinett.

9–15. Drawings for The Battle of Cascina.— The most important of the works commissioned from Michelangelo after his return to Florence in 1501 was, without a doubt, the great fresco that was to occupy the left section of the east wall of the Sala del Consiglio in the Palazzo Vecchio. The decoration of the right section was entrusted to Leonardo in October 1503.

It is not known exactly when the *gonfaloniere* Pier Soderini gave the commission to Michelangelo but it is known that the artist worked on the cartoon in December 1504 and that at the end of February 1505, just before he left for Rome at the invitation of Julius II, who intended to entrust him with the design and execution of his tomb, Michelangelo received an advance payment for the actual painting of the fresco in the Palazzo Vecchio, a job that he could have just barely begun. At this time the cartoon was most probably finished. The subject chosen by Michelangelo to honor the Republic of Florence was the battle won by the Florentines against the Pisans near Cascina in July 1364. Leonardo had chosen the battle of Anghiari, fought successfully against the Visconti in 1440. The center of Michelangelo's composition was to have been a group of soldiers surprised by the alarm brought to the Florentine camp by Manno Donati. This episode is documented in the grisaille copy of the cartoon in the collection of Lord Leicester at Holkham Hall. It is possible that there were other scenes planned for the fresco. A fight between mounted soldiers or between foot and cavalry may have been one of the scenes to be included. Both Vasari's description of the cartoon and several drawings datable to this period suggest this. The cartoon itself has been lost. Michelangelo drew it in the Ospedale dei Tintori. It was then taken to the Sala del Consiglio and from there transported to the Sala del Papa near Santa Maria Novella. Later it was brought to the Palazzo Medici, where about 1515 or 1516, according to Vasari, it was divided and the pieces were dispersed.

"While they still existed, they were a school of the world," proclaimed Cellini apropos of the cartoons by Leonardo and Michelangelo. They were lauded, studied and copied by almost every artist who had the good fortune to see them. Yet only a few drawings remain to preserve the cartoons for us.

According to Vasari, Michelangelo used a number of techniques to sketch the figures in his cartoon: "some [were] outlined in black chalk, some drawn with line and others made from shadow and white lead highlights." We recognize this variety in part even in the drawings, where the soft stroke of chalk alternates with the sharp line of the pen. The use of chalk becomes more frequent from this point on in the drawings of Michelangelo, permitting subtle variations of dark and light on the surfaces of the figures that correspond to the more complex problems of movement that the artist posed for himself in these Florentine years. Each figure is frozen in the momentary instability of a movement. The curved lines that outline the figures emphasize the tension of the great muscles contracted in a strain that precedes action. From this one gets the impression that tremendous energy is generated by, and contained within, these individuals of monumental size and proportion.

9. This sketch for a cavalry battle in pen line and without shading seems to have been inspired by contemporaneous studies by Leonardo for *The Battle of Anghiari* and must refer to an episode that the artist intended to introduce into the fresco in the Palazzo Vecchio. The two erect figures on the right and the left of the page are definitely connected with the statues of the twelve Apostles commissioned from Michelangelo by the Opera of the cathedral in April 1503. Of these statues Michelangelo began only the *St. Matthew* (Florence, Accademia), which he worked on in May 1506. This does not exclude the possibility that he had started it some time before, as a document of payment dated 1504 (Brugnoli) seems to suggest. If one wishes to relate these two sketches to the *St. Matthew* one must imagine an earlier and completely different idea than the one worked on in marble. While the figure in the drawing appears static and perfectly balanced, the *St. Matthew* of the Accademia is presented in a state of spiritual agony that is expressed by a tortured structure of the limbs foreshadowing the most dramatic expressions of Michelangelo's art.

London, British Museum, 1895-9-15-469 *recto*; pen and ink, 186 × 183 mm; British Museum photo.

10. Young Male Nude.—The memory of the *Apollo Belvedere* that the artist had the opportunity to see in the Palazzo della Rovere during his first sojourn in Rome seems to

have inspired Michelangelo in this beautiful drawing. The technique of crosshatched pen lines achieves a masterly perfection in the suggestion of the psychology of the subject and the definition of the admirable modeling of the torso, which makes Michelangelo's figure much more lifelike than the ancient statue. If this drawing has no direct connection with the cartoon for *The Battle of Cascina* it certainly does originate in the same period of Michelangelo's activity. The artist reworked this figure in the drawing reproduced in Plate 11.

London, British Museum, 1887-5-2-117 *recto*; pen and ink, 375 × 230 mm; British Museum photo.

11. Studies of Figures and The Madonna of Bruges.—The group, which does not appear in the incomplete copy of the cartoon today at Holkham Hall, must have been conceived for the composition of the *Battle*, and the artist probably intended to represent by it Manno Donati in the act of giving the alarm in the Florentine camp. The nude young warrior in full front view echoes the preceding drawing in the gesture of the left arm and the slant of the torso. The use of soft chalk produces an ample modeling effectively suggestive of sculpture in the round.

The pen sketch for *The Madonna of Bruges* is difficult to consider as a sketch after the statue (Tolnay). It may, therefore, be considered to confirm the dating of the group to around 1504.

London, British Museum, 1859-6-25-564 *recto*; black chalk and pen and ink, 315 × 278 mm; Alinari photo.

12. Studies of Figures.—This is the most complete extant study for the composition of the group known as the "Bathers." We can recognize it, despite numerous variations, in the Holkham Hall copy of the *Battle* cartoon. It has often been a matter of dispute among critics, and only recently has its authenticity been established (Barocchi). The rapid and summary definition of the group makes one think of a preliminary sketch intended to be reworked and changed. That some of these figures, which do not appear in the Holkham copy, were to have been placed in the fresco is proved by the following drawing of a nude from the Casa Buonarroti.

Florence, Uffizi, 613 E *recto*; black chalk and silverpoint, 235 × 356 mm; Alinari photo.

13 & 14. Nudes.—These are two finished drawings for the "Bathers." The first nude is the final version of the figure with a raised shoulder, the fourth figure from the left, in Plate 12. The second, seated on the shore and turned toward the right, is also easily recognizable in the Holkham Hall copy.

Because of their high level of finish these drawings must be placed among the latest of the drawings for the *Battle* and are therefore datable to the end of 1504 or the beginning of 1505. Some critics have judged them to be copies or even forgeries, but to us, on the contrary, they present two examples, certainly not isolated, of the way Michelangelo executed the *modelli* for his works, obtaining with just the use of the black-and-white medium the sculptural effects he later translated into marble or paint.

Florence, Casa Buonarroti, 73 F *recto*; pen and ink and traces of black chalk, 408 × 284 mm; Alinari photo.

London, British Museum, 1887-5-2-116 *recto*; pen and ink and brush with touches of white lead, 421 × 287 mm; Alinari photo.

15. Skirmish between Cavalry and Foot Soldiers. —This is one of the drawings of which the chronology is most uncertain. Most critics relate it to *The Battle of Cascina*, while others associate it with the Medici Chapel, a difference in period of more than twenty years.

The subject is analogous to that of Plate 9, and is also similar to another drawing in the Ashmolean Museum (Robinson 18 *recto*). The three compositions—connected by a common inspiration, Leonardo's *Battle of Anghiari*—seem to us to be very difficult to separate from *The Battle of Cascina* project, which depicted, according to Vasari, "many warriors fighting on horseback opening the skirmish."

This presentation of the theme, more complex than in the other two drawings, makes one think of the next step in Michelangelo's development, in which the problem of movement, of constantly increasing importance to the artist throughout the period of his work on the *Battle* cartoon, begins to resolve itself in terms of dramatic violence. Nor is the style of modeling, with broad strokes of the pen, in discord with the drawings of this period.

A subsequent version of a "battle between cavalry and foot soldiers" can be recognized in the medallion supported by the two nudes at the left of *The Creation of Eve* in the Sistine ceiling.

Oxford, Ashmolean Museum, Robinson 16; pen and ink, 179 × 251 mm; Ashmolean Museum photo.

16. Study of a Nude.—Michelangelo's frequent reworkings of the same type of figure, sometimes years apart, render problematic the dating of this drawing and the one that follows. There is a similarity between the tormented figure in this Louvre drawing and the crucified Haman in one of the angular compartments of the Sistine ceiling. The *Haman* belongs to an advanced phase of the artist's work on that project, and so a dating of about 1511 has been proposed. But one can also point to a relationship between this drawing and the *Captives* conceived for the tomb of Julius II as early as the first design of 1505, or the *St. Matthew,* on which Michelangelo was still working in May 1506. We are dealing with a nude study in which Michelangelo's inner conflict is expressed in the most appropriate and congenial terms. The Hellenistic influences, whether Rhodian or Pergamene, which appear in this sketch (there has been an attempt to establish a connection between this sketch and the *Laocoön,* rediscovered on the Esquiline hill in January 1506), should be understood as the forms which the artist adopted *a posteriori* to express his inspiration rather than as the inspiration itself.

The recognition that the drawing of the arm and the sketch of the old man on the right of this sheet are, respectively, a study for the *St. Matthew* and an early idea for the *Moses* on the tomb of Julius II has led to a dating of this drawing around 1506. In fact, this study of the nude offers, in comparison with the *Haman,* a more slender representation of the body that is nearer to the style of the Florentine years than to the later period of the Sistine Chapel.

Paris, Louvre, R. F. 1068 *recto*; pen and ink, 340 × 168 mm; Louvre photo.

17. Madonna and Child with St. Anne.—In this case also, similarities are easily found with figures from the Sistine ceiling. The figure of the woman in the *Ozias* triangle is presented in the same way as the St. Anne. In the Madonna nursing her Son, Michelangelo reworks a theme already treated in drawings of the Florentine years of the Pitti and Taddei *tondi,* a theme which will be applied again to the Medici *Madonna.*

The decisive stroke of the pen and the energetic opposition of dark and light create a plastic effect not unlike the last drawings for the cartoon of *The Battle of Cascina,* suggesting a date for the drawing immediately preceding the Sistine ceiling rather than about 1510, which would be the date if it were considered as a preparatory drawing for the *Ozias.* The nude at the bottom of the page is perhaps another study of David, more virile than the drawing for the bronze *David* or the Florentine statue and thus suggesting, even more than the marble statue in the Piazza della Signoria, how classical and Biblical symbols of strength, Hercules and David, were fused in the artist's mind (Tolnay).

Paris, Louvre, 685 *recto*; pen and ink, 325 × 260 mm; Alinari photo.

18-25. Drawings for the Ceiling of the Sistine Chapel.—Pope Julius II must have offered the commission for the decoration of the Sistine ceiling to Michelangelo in the same period, between March 1505 and April 1506, in which the artist began the work on the Papal tomb. He refused the commission at that time. It took a brief by the imperious pontiff two years later to overcome his reluctance. It was to be a tremendous task—the chapel measures 40 meters long by 13 wide—and to Michelangelo, the sculptor, painting seemed extraneous to his own artistic activity. In a letter to his father Ludovico dated January 1509, the artist, expressing his dissatisfaction with the way the work on the frescoes was proceeding, declared, "and this is the difficulty with the work, that it is not my profession."

In May 1508, however, the contract was drawn up and Michelangelo started on the great work which he did not finish until early October of 1512. At the hour of Vespers on October 31, the eve of All Saints' Day, the frescoes were solemnly unveiled in the presence of Julius II.

The tremendous work, executed during four years of great labor almost completely by the master's own hand—the role of helpers and apprentices was limited to minor portions—was complete. Never has an artist's uncertainty or hesitancy been less justified. In the Sistine ceiling Michelangelo, by this time in his full maturity, has left to mankind one of the greatest artistic achievements of all time. Vasari said of it, "Lamp of our art . . . bright enough to illuminate the world," and this is certainly not empty hyperbole.

The subjects of the frescoes, starting from the lowest zone, the lunettes, and proceeding around and upward toward the center of the ceiling, are: *Forebears of Christ* (or *Patriarchs*), the *Prophets* and the *Sibyls*, the *ignudi* and nine stories from Genesis—from the *Separation of Light from Darkness* to the *Drunkenness of Noah*. The artist created a whole superhuman world which was defined in terms of the Neoplatonic doctrines current in Florence at the end of the fifteenth century, which Michelangelo made his own to the extent that they responded to his own deep understanding of the human condition. For Michelangelo this was an expression of the possibilities implicit in man for dominating the material substance which imprisons the soul and allowing the soul, as a thing divine, to ascend to its Creator.

From God to man, from the Creator to His creation. The process can also be inverted: from a humanity abandoned to its most unhappy earthly condition (the *Patriarchs* in the lunettes and triangles), through the contemplation and revelation expressed in the *Prophets* and *Sibyls*, we arrive at the sole Principle of the Created Being. Man lives by the will of God, but if under the pressure of desires of the flesh he forgets his origins he will fall to the level of the brute. The *Drunkenness of Noah*, the last of the episodes on the ceiling, is a symbol of this and a warning.

In the conception and the execution of the frescoes Michelangelo did not follow the order suggested by the subjects which he treated. He must have started with the part of the ceiling next to the entrance wall and proceeded toward the altar wall, reserving for last the lunettes and the segments that contain the *Patriarchs*. A better indication of this progression than the few imprecise extant documents on this matter is the style of the frescoes, which develops in the direction of a greater breadth of composition and greater complexity in the use of color as one proceeds toward the back wall of the Chapel.

Relatively few drawings for the project, considering its great size, remain to us. No cartoon has been preserved and the sketches and studies which can be firmly related to the ceiling are very few. This is another example of the unfortunate dispersion of the graphic production of the artist, due in part to Michelangelo's own desire and in a much greater measure to the negligence of the men who inherited the drawings.

18. This sketch refers to an earlier project for the ceiling that was to be limited, according to the information we have from Michelangelo himself (in a letter of December 1523 to Giovanni Fattucci), to "the twelve Apostles in the lunettes and the rest made up of partitions filled with decoration." The effect was judged to be a "poor thing" by the artist himself, and so Julius II redefined his instructions, allowing Michelangelo to do as he saw fit.

In this sketch Michelangelo adopted a type of coffering which occurs in Tuscan architecture of the late fifteenth century. He later substituted for this a broad system of bands, cornices and pilasters that underline the powerful tension of the massive masonry of the vaulted ceiling and at the same time share the taut restlessness of the figures that people this construction. The sketches of arms and hands belong to a later period. They are studies that the artist used with varying degrees of change in some of the figures for the ceiling.

London, British Museum, 1859-6-25-567 *recto*; pen and ink and black chalk, 275 × 386 mm; British Museum photo.

19. Study for the Adam in The Expulsion from Paradise.—The authenticity and identification of this study have been unjustly questioned. The few lines which describe the structure of the anatomy catch the figure in the most violent part of an action and right before our eyes seem to translate the first ideas from the artist's mind into visual images.

Florence, Casa Buonarroti, 45 F; black chalk, 262 × 191 mm; Alinari photo.

20 & 21. Studies of Heads.—These studies are variously connected with different figures in the ceiling. Analogies have been suggested between the head of the young man and several of the *ignudi* and the Adam in *The Creation*. The head of the old man has been identified as a portrait of Pope Julius II and also as a study for *Zacharias* or *Ezekiel*. Perhaps these

drawings should instead be considered examples of the artist's ideal of beauty in his early maturity. Both of them are very noble and could have been drawn from a live model (in the case of the old man the inspiration could very well have come from the imperious face of the Pope) and then reworked into an ideal type that in the young man reaches a Greek purity. The head of the young man is repeated with little variation in many of the figures of the ceiling. The intensely introspective head of the old man, on the other hand, besides recalling some of the Prophets, foreshadows the head of the statue of Moses.

Florence, Uffizi, 18718 F *recto*; black chalk, 432 × 280 mm; Alinari photo.

London, British Museum, 1895-9-15-498 *verso*; red and black chalk and pen and ink, 331 × 215 mm; Alinari photo.

22. Study of a Nude.—Probably for the *ignudo* to the right of the Prophet *Isaiah*. This is one of the rare cases in which Michelangelo used silverpoint. Even in this medium, very common during the Renaissance but not well suited to the representation of the robust modeling of the ceiling figures, the artist is able to achieve an exceptional relief-like quality in the powerful musculature and to invest the figures, by the subtle manipulation of chiaroscuro, with a pulsing vitality. The *ignudi*, interpretable in Neoplatonic terms as symbols of human reason, reflect many reminiscences of ancient work, coming either from Hellenistic statuary or the Medici gems. The Antique, however, is always fused with nature and is never the formative influence.

Florence, Uffizi, 1870 F *recto*; silverpoint, 420 × 265 mm; Alinari photo.

23. Study of a Head.—The chronology of this drawing is often a matter for dispute, but never its excellent quality. The facial characteristics coincide with both those of the Madonna in the Doni *tondo* and with the *Jonah* on the Sistine ceiling. More than five years separated these two works, and so to relate the drawing to one of them rather than the other displaces the date of the drawing by that much time. The *Jonah*, in fact, belongs to the last period of the artist's work on the ceiling and can be dated about 1511. The drawing seems to suggest precisely this final period of work in the Sistine Chapel because

of the trembling and enveloping light falling on the surface of the forms that replaces the sharp sculptural definition of earlier sheets.

Florence, Casa Buonarroti, 1 F *recto*; red chalk, 199 × 172 mm; Alinari photo.

24 & 25. These are drawings in red chalk, among the most finished of those which have come down to us from these years, for the *Libyan Sibyl* and for the sprite (*genietto*) at the left. They are studies from life. The young male nude of the Metropolitan Museum sheet will be transformed into the female figure of the *Sibyl*, once again demonstrating the relative unimportance that the models, live and Antique, had in the definition of the Michelangelesque ideal figure. The soft transition from light to dark, especially in the Metropolitan Museum drawing, attests to the full maturity as a painter that the artist developed in the Sistine ceiling project. He makes use of this soft chiaroscuro to produce the energetic tension of the anatomical structure, which is underlined by the firm and leaping stroke that surrounds it.

Both of these drawings are of excellent quality and are datable around 1511. Our interest in the Oxford sheet is increased by the presence of six pen sketches for the *Captives* of the tomb of Julius II, which are the most important of the few figure drawings which can be related to that project. The motif of figures chained to the pillars of the base of the sepulchre (the Provinces subjugated by the Pope, according to Vasari; the Liberal Arts and the Plastic Arts, according to Condivi) already appears in the first project for the tomb (1505) and reappears, with more violently tormented poses, in the second project, 1513. The Oxford sketches, because of the dramatic significance that the *contrapposto* of the figures assumes, remind one of this second project and of the two *Captives* executed in 1513, now in the Louvre. These sketches were probably influenced by the motif introduced by Leonardo in his drawings for the Trivulzio monument (Brugnoli).

The theme of the irreconcilable conflict between spiritual force and inert matter is presented in these six sketches with a decisiveness that makes it clear that the terms and the solution of the problem were well defined in the mind of the artist. The last *ignudi* of the ceiling are contorted in the same struggle as these *Captives* and so it is not necessary (even if the possibility is not to be excluded) to suppose that the six figures in pen and ink were added to the Oxford sheet at a later date.

The sketches of a female head and a male torso at the left of the Metropolitan Museum sheet were probably done by another hand.

New York, Metropolitan Museum, 24-197-2 *recto*; red chalk, 289 × 214 mm; Metropolitan Museum photo.

Oxford, Ashmolean Museum, Robinson 23 *recto*; red chalk and pen and ink, 286 × 194 mm; Ashmolean Museum photo.

26. Study for a Prophet (?).—This study was formerly referred to the Prophets and Sibyls of the Sistine ceiling. It was then correctly redated by Wilde to the years when Michelangelo was working in the Medici Chapel. The identification of the architectural drawing in the background as a plan, never carried out, for the choir loft of the chapel suggests a dating before 1524. The figure, not clearly identifiable, but more female than male, shows, in the elaborate S-curved composition, the motif that will characterize the Medici *Madonna*. The crosshatching of the pen lines is reminiscent of the early drawings, but the powerful sculptural effects of those drawings are enriched here with more complex variations of light and shadow.

London, British Museum, 1887-5-2-115; pen and ink, 414 × 281 mm; British Museum photo.

27. Study of a Female Head.—This drawing, like the preceding one, has been connected with the figures in the Sistine ceiling, but it is more probable that it was done a short time before the first statues for the Medici tombs. The fluid shading of the face is in fact more reminiscent of the drawing of the head in the Casa Buonarroti 7 F (Plate 35), whose intent thoughtfulness and intimate solitude this beautiful drawing shares, than of the drawing of Jonah (Plate 23). Perhaps it is possible to identify this drawing as one of those "divine heads" that Michelangelo drew for his dearest friends and which are mentioned for the first time by Vasari in relation to the "three sheets" given by the artist "to Gherardo Perini, a Florentine gentleman," with whom Michelangelo was friendly about 1522.

Oxford, Ashmolean Museum, Robinson 10; red chalk, 205 × 165 mm; Ashmolean Museum photo.

28–31. Drawings for the Medici Chapel.—In the body of the surviving Michelangelo drawings those referring to the statuary and the decoration of the Medici Chapel are extremely rare, and many of them are problematic as to their authenticity and chronology.

Michelangelo was engaged in the work on the Chapel in San Lorenzo, the "New Sacristy," for about fifteen years, a period of time which runs from his full maturity to the beginning of his old age. Because of the momentous historic events of the time and the difficulties which he ran up against in his many artistic activities, this was certainly the most strife-ridden period of Michelangelo's life. The projects with which he was occupied, all of such great importance that they would have made the hand of a lesser man tremble, were commissioned by the most powerful political figures of the time. In the end the projects themselves became involved in the conflicts and rivalries that overwhelmed the men who commissioned them.

The job of designing and constructing the chapel in San Lorenzo and the tombs for four members of the Medici house (Lorenzo the Magnificent; his brother Giuliano; Lorenzo, Duke of Urbino; and Giuliano, Duke of Nemours) was entrusted to Michelangelo in 1520 by Leo X and Cardinal Giulio de' Medici. In September 1534, when Michelangelo left Florence permanently for Rome, the grandiose project was not yet completed. The four allegorical statues (*Night*, *Day*, *Morning* and *Evening*), the two statues of Dukes Lorenzo and Giuliano and the statue of the Madonna and Child were finished, but the allegorical statues had not yet been mounted over the sarcophagi, and the sarcophagus for Lorenzo the Magnificent and his brother Giuliano, above which the Madonna and Child and the statues of Sts. Cosmas and Damian (by Montorsoli and Raffaello da Montelupo, respectively) were to be placed, was still missing.

The sack of Rome in 1527 and the consequent exile of the Medici from Florence, as well as the conflict between the new Florentine Republic and the Papacy, in which Michelangelo sided with the Florentines, thereby provoking the anger of the new Medici Pope, Clement VII, interrupted for more than three years the work on the Chapel. In addition to the Medici Chapel and the huge tomb of Pope Julius II, commissions for a *Hercules* to be placed in the Piazza della Signoria, for three paintings—*Leda, Venus and Cupid* and a *Noli Me Tangere*—and for the Laurentian Library had been added to Michelangelo's burden. A tremendous amount of work, honestly too much for any one man, so it is no wonder that some works remained unfinished or were not completed after the original plan.

Among these works it is the Medici Chapel that gives us the most exact measure of the level of Michelangelo's achievement as an architect and a sculptor in his late maturity. Since the scope of the project for the tomb of Julius II in San Pietro in Vincoli was reduced through many transformations to a mere shadow of the vast original plan, the funeral chapel in San Lorenzo is the only remaining example of the supreme balance of architecture and sculpture—producing an effect of awesome monumental unity—of which the genius of Michelangelo was capable.

28. These are quick sketches, limited to essential lines, for one of the reclining figures of the four Rivers that were to be placed two by two under the sarcophagi of Dukes Giuliano and Lorenzo. The four statues were never executed in marble, but Michelangelo did do models of them in "*terra di cimatura*." One of these models is commonly recognized in the terracotta figure in the Accademia of Florence. From such models, probably, the artist obtained the measurements for the block of marble from which the figures were to be cut. Since the marble for the *River Gods* (perhaps the four rivers of Hades) was cut from the Apuan Mountains during the late summer and early autumn of 1525, this date establishes a *terminus ante quem* for this sketch, which was evidently intended for the stonecutter.

The extreme economy of the stroke creates in a few lines of force the scale and proportions of the figure, more elongated than in preceding works and of a more concentrated energy that implies a sense of renunciation and abandonment, the same quality we find in the Medici Chapel statues. It is suggested here with such clarity of purpose that it makes one mourn the many "work" sketches that have

been lost forever. From the measurements jotted down on the sketch we know that the finished figures were to have been about twice life size.

London, British Museum, 1859-6-25-544 *recto*; pen and ink, 137 × 209 mm; British Museum photo.

29. Anatomical studies form a small part of Michelangelo's drawings, especially when compared to the number done by Leonardo; this was a result of the different attitudes of the two artists. Leonardo regarded detailed research into the facts of nature the necessary foundation for the "experimental method" which allowed him to rise from the world of phenomena to the one and supreme Reason which governs all things. To Michelangelo, on the other hand, the study of the skeleton, muscles and tendons had only a relative and always subordinate importance, demonstrating the violence implicit in the aspects of nature. This study of legs (the motif was of classical origin and was a favorite of Michelangelo's during the Medici Chapel period) reappears with little variation in the statue of *Night* and in the *River Gods* and also in the painting of *Leda* commissioned by Duke Alfonso d'Este in July 1529 and finished by October 1530. This painting was entrusted by the artist in 1531, along with the cartoon for it, to the apprentice Antonio Mini, who took it to France. Both the painting and the cartoon were later lost. We know the composition, however, through copies.

Florence, Casa Buonarroti, 44 F; pen and ink, 145 × 193 mm; Alinari photo.

30. Grotesque Heads.—These three drawings have been connected both with the grotesque masks in the frieze behind the allegorical figures of the tombs of the Dukes and with those in the capitals of the pilasters that flank the niches containing the statues of Giuliano and Lorenzo. Partially because of the sketch of *Hercules and Antaeus* which appears to the right of the heads, the sheet is to be dated around 1525. The three heads, however, bear only a generic likeness to the masks in the Medici frieze. They seem rather to be physiognomic studies (as Wittkower noted) of a brutalized humanity, in which the physical features—the harelip of the young man and the long ears and satyr's horns of the old men

—apparently are intended to depict full moral decadence. There is some similarity with Leonardo in the sketch of the old man at the bottom that is reminiscent of the famous "*schiaccianoci*" (nutcracker). But instead of an acute curiosity about natural phenomena the drawings show a desire to deform the face to emphasize dramatic qualities.

The sketch on the right at the bottom of the sheet is for a *Hercules and Antaeus*, probably the statuary group to be placed in the Piazza della Signoria, the first idea for which stems from 1508. At that time the subject was probably *Hercules and Cacus*, but in the summer of 1525, when the commission was returned to Michelangelo, he changed it to a *Hercules and Antaeus*. The commission was later given to Bandinelli at the command of the Medici, and the statue was placed in front of the Palazzo Vecchio in 1534.

The intricate composition of the two entwined nudes recalls ancient statuary groups well known even to the artists of the fifteenth century. New is the wildly struggling nude figure of Antaeus which welds itself to the figure of Hercules with a quivering fury that brings to mind Michelangelo's theory, reported by Lomazzo, for composing the *figura serpentinata* in the fashion of a "tongue of flame."

London, British Museum, 1859-6-25-557 *recto*; red chalk, 255 × 350 mm; Alinari photo.

31. Drawings of animals by Michelangelo are very rare. His interests usually centered around the human figure. This pen drawing, of a fineness of line that recalls the drawings of the pre-Sistine ceiling period, presents in the entwined, elongated and sinuous body a heraldic elegance that well conforms with the style of the Medici Chapel period. The figure was perhaps intended for the bases of the candelabra on the altar of the Chapel (Berenson). The design of a monstrous figure which actually appears there is a simpler and more traditional one.

The profile sketches were done by a pupil.
Oxford, Ashmolean Museum, Robinson 13 *recto*; pen and ink, 254 × 338 mm; Ashmolean Museum photo.

32 & 33. Studies for a Madonna and Child and for a Holy Family.—These two drawings, both of good quality, are datable to the period of activity in the chapel in San Lorenzo, even though, with a difference of more than five years between the first and the second one, they cannot be considered preparatory studies for the Medici *Madonna*, but should be understood as elaborations of a theme that had fascinated the artist since the years of his second sojourn in Florence (*cf.* Plate 17) and that achieved a monumental conclusion in the marble group. The statue of the *Madonna and Child* was the one on which the artist worked the longest. In April 1521 the marble was cut from the mountain at Carrara and in September 1531 the statue was still unfinished. It is not surprising, therefore, that in these years Michelangelo studied various solutions of the theme of the Madonna nursing her Child. It is also possible that other works on the same theme may have been requested from him in the years around 1522 (Wilde).

In the Casa Buonarroti drawing the "heroic" pose of the Madonna recalls the *Sibyls* of the Sistine ceiling, but in the caressing chiaroscuro of the figure of the Child there is already the subtle luminous quality of the translucent surface of the *Night*. The figure in the London drawing, where the position of the lower part of the figure is similar to that of the *Duke Giuliano* (Tolnay), is closer to the Medici *Madonna*. The very fluid and enveloping shadows reduce the energy of the muscular mass and accentuate the feeling of the weight of the body. This effect seems to have been reproduced in the marble group by the intentional prominence of the chisel marks on the surface.

Florence, Casa Buonarroti, 71 F; black, red and white chalk, 541 × 396 mm; Alinari photo.

London, British Museum, Pp. 1-58; black chalk, 317 × 191 mm; British Museum photo.

34 & 35. These two red chalk heads, not necessarily connected with any definite work in marble or oil, are fine examples of those studies in which the artist, motivated by a passionate and always renewed desire to investigate the human form, distilled from the live model the most significant and essential lines in order to confer a universal meaning on the individual. The head of the young man has an arrogant vitality that is underlined by the strong features. At the same time it

demonstrates, by the ironic line of the lip and the wide-open eye, a pathetic knowledge of defeat. This dramatic image is best connected with the years of the artist's late maturity.

The same can be said of the head of the young woman with an absorbed expression. There is a happy union of both vigorous elements (the individualized strokes) and delicate ones (the graduated continuity of the surfaces). This feminine type is also found in the *Patriarchs* of the Sistine ceiling and was reworked in the Medici statues and in the *Leda*. The drawing has been, in fact, related to the painting for Alfonso d'Este. At any rate it must be dated to the last years of Michelangelo's activity in the Medici Chapel.

Oxford, Ashmolean Museum, Robinson 9; red chalk, 282 × 198 mm; Ashmolean Museum photo.

Florence, Casa Buonarroti, 7 F; red chalk, 354 × 269 mm; Alinari photo.

36–38. Studies for an Adoration of the Bronze Serpent and a Resurrection.—Since, for reasons of style, the first drawing could not relate to the fresco of the same subject in one of the angular areas of the Sistine ceiling, we know of no work with which these drawings could be connected. It has been supposed (Popp) that Michelangelo planned to paint scenes depicting the brazen serpent and the Resurrection, symbolizing the punishment of sin and the hope of salvation in God, in the lunettes above the Medici tombs, but there are no documents to prove this hypothesis.

The stylistic character of the drawings, however, makes a dating to the last years of Michelangelo's presence in Florence very probable.

In *The Adoration of the Bronze Serpent* (Plate 36) the Biblical story (Numbers 21: 6–9) is told in terms of tragic violence. Figural motifs already studied at the time of the cartoon for *The Battle of Cascina* (*cf.* Plates 11 and 15) are presented here with a dramatic excitement that foreshadows the *Last Judgment* in the Sistine Chapel. The articulation of the nude figures is done rapidly and allusively with an increasingly diffused shadow. The individual is blended into a mob swept by a common desperate terror. The Christian sense of guilt and sin weighs heavily on the mind of the artist, and the hope of divine salvation overrides every human potentiality.

The high column supporting the bronze serpent, barely indicated to the left of the upper group, leads to the supposition that the composition did not contain a symmetric group on the right (Parker) and that the group of figures apparently reaching for the symbol of salvation, for which the drawing on the lower part of our sheet is a study, would have been located on a second level, beside the statue of the serpent. The hope of salvation, expressed in Old Testament terms in *The Adoration of the Bronze Serpent*, is made more specifically Christian and more explicit in the two drawings of *The Resurrection* (37 and 38), where the eternal dualism of spirit and matter takes on a paradigmatic clarity. The Christ, an athletic nude of unrestrained vigor that does not have its source in the strength of the anatomical structure, springs from the prison of the sepulcher and hovers in the air, now an image of pure spiritual beauty, freed from all earthly ties. Contrasted to this is the very human terror of the guards, whose senses have been overwhelmed by the event they have witnessed, and who are imprisoned without hope in the corruptible matter of their bodies.

Black chalk, used with supreme mastery of chiaroscuro in both the Windsor and the London sheets (the London drawing was done slightly later), proves to be a medium extremely well adapted to the presentation of Michelangelesque images. With it the artist obtained an effect of extreme plasticity and at the same time a soft diffusion of light and dark. This is particularly apparent in the figure of the London Christ, where the intense luminosity of the body makes us sensitive to the purely spiritual significance of the image, whose refined form has a Hellenic harmony.

Oxford, Ashmolean Museum, Robinson 29; red chalk, 244 × 335 mm; Ashmolean Museum photo.

Windsor Castle, Royal Collection, 12767 *recto*; black chalk, 240 × 347 mm; Windsor photo (reproduced with the kind permission of H.M. Queen Elizabeth II).

London, British Museum, 1860-6-16-133; black chalk, 326 × 286 mm; Alinari photo.

39. Study for a Resurrected Christ.—Many other drawings (Casa Buonarroti; Ashmolean Museum; Windsor, 12771 *verso*; British Museum)

of the same subject, all datable around 1532, have been preserved, but none of them is as highly finished as this nude, which exhibits a renewed classicism that places it close to the drawings for Tommaso Cavalieri. The figure of Christ, related to a *Resurrection* like Plate 37 and characterized by the energy of the broad modeling of the limbs, offers more than one analogy with the Zeus in the *Fall of Phaëthon* and the Christ of the Sistine *Last Judgment*. Berenson, often very cautious in judging the more finished drawings of Michelangelo, considered the Windsor sheet to be one of the greatest master drawings of all time.

Windsor Castle, Royal Collection, 12768; black chalk, 373 × 221 mm; Windsor photo (reproduced with the kind permission of H.M. Queen Elizabeth II).

40. This pen sketch exemplifies a rapid and abbreviated method of drawing used by Michelangelo to jot down the tumult of ideas as they came into his mind, a method completely different from the finished style of the preceding drawing. It is one of a series of six sheets in the Casa Buonarroti whose subject and dating are much discussed. The most widely accepted hypothesis is that they are the sketches which Vasari reports that Michelangelo did for the *Martyrdom of St. Catherine* that his friend Giuliano Bugiardini painted for the Rucellai family. But in reality none of the groups of figures in the panel in Santa Maria Novella has more than a generic similarity to these sketches. Nevertheless, the most probable dating is around 1532.

Florence, Casa Buonarroti, 67 F; pen and ink, 110 × 116 mm; photo by Sopr. Gallerie, Florence.

41. Sacrifice of Isaac.—Only recently has the high quality of this drawing been recognized (Barocchi). The group has an exemplary monumental unity created by the cohesive formal relationship between Abraham and the young Isaac. Because of the dramatic impact of the gesture of Abraham about to strike his son and of the angel who restrains him at the last minute, the drawing brings to mind the panel Brunelleschi did in competition with Ghiberti at the beginning of the fifteenth century. The analogous tension of human relationships among the characters of one of the most dramatic stories in the Bible suggests that Michelangelo was also thinking of the Brunelleschi work. The writhing struggle of the nude Isaac, underlined by the relentless repetition of the curved outlines, recalls the *Captives* in the Accademia in Florence, which, with this drawing, can probably be dated to the period immediately preceding the *Last Judgment* of the Sistine Chapel.

Florence, Casa Buonarroti, 70 F; black and red chalk and pen and ink, 408 × 289 mm; Alinari photo.

42 & 43. Tityus; Fall of Phaëthon.—Vasari notes four mythological compositions (the *Ganymede*, the *Tityus*, the *Phaëthon* and a *Bacchanal of Children*) among the drawings done by Michelangelo for Tommaso Cavalieri to help his young friend "learn to draw." The meeting between Michelangelo, already on the verge of old age, and the Roman nobleman must have occurred in Rome at the end of 1532. The tenacious and passionate friendship which it began lasted to the end of the artist's life.

Two of the drawings, most likely the *Ganymede* and the *Tityus*, were already in the possession of Cavalieri in January 1533. The first of the three versions of *The Fall of Phaëthon* (the London sheet) was sent to him before Michelangelo left Rome for Florence in June of that year. The *Tityus* and *Phaëthon* drawings, therefore, are among the very few sheets that can be dated with almost complete certainty to a specific year.

In the drawings for Cavalieri a more precisely definable use of ancient art coincides with the classical subject matter inspired by mythology and the stories of Ovid. There is a care of execution in these drawings that was greatly admired by Michelangelo's contemporaries (Vasari wrote, "it would be impossible to achieve greater harmony of texture and light"), but that has been less well received by some modern critics (Berenson).

The first three subjects have been rightly interpreted in Neoplatonic terms (Panofsky, *Studies*) as symbols of the ecstasy of Platonic love (*Ganymede*—the original drawing has been lost), of the torment of sensual passion that enslaves the soul (*Tityus*) and of the destiny of the presumptuous (*Phaëthon*). The sin of presumptuousness is one of which Michelangelo accuses himself in letters to Cavalieri.

It is probably in this friendship between Michelangelo and the young Roman nobleman, characterized by an atmosphere of exaggerated idealization of human sentiments, that we must seek the reasons for this brief period of renewed classicism that attempts to reaffirm the divine quality of earthly beauty.

Of the three versions of the myth of Phaëthon (the other two are in the Accademia of Venice and at Windsor) the London drawing in particular has the character of a first idea, and for that reason it is less completely finished than the Windsor drawing. But the dramatic violence is greater, especially in the group of the Heliades depicted in the moment of transformation from human into inanimate forms.

At the bottom of the sheet is the message that accompanied the drawing when it was brought to Michelangelo's friend by the apprentice Urbino.

Windsor Castle, Royal Collection, 12771 *recto*; black chalk, 190 × 330 mm; Windsor photo (reproduced with the kind permission of H.M. Queen Elizabeth II).

London, British Museum, 1895-9-15-517; black chalk, 313 × 217 mm; British Museum photo.

44. The Archers.—This is one of the drawings whose subject and authorship are most discussed. The identification of the literary source for the drawing in the *Nigrinus* of Lucian or in a passage from Pico della Mirandola (Panofsky, *Studies*) are both credible, but arguable. A more persuasive hypothesis is that the idea for the composition came from a stucco which decorated the ceiling of a room in Nero's Domus Aurea and which is recognizable in a watercolor by Francisco de Hollanda, author of the *Dialogues* in which Michelangelo is introduced as the main speaker.

Doubts as to the authorship of the drawing were primarily aroused by the presence on the verso of an inscription of the late sixteenth century that would indicate the artist as Giulio Clovio. But the quality of the drawing is such as to make one at least cautious in accepting this attribution. The perfect harmony of the young male nudes and the fluidity of the form-modeling chiaroscuro that allies itself with the tension of the lines, relate this drawing to those done for Cavalieri. Even if we do not have documentation for a drawing of this subject for the Roman

nobleman, the sheet should be dated in those same years. The widespread fame of this drawing among Michelangelo's contemporaries is confirmed by a fresco of the school of Raphael, today in the Borghese Gallery (No. 294).

The sheet has been cut on the extreme right and left sides.

Windsor Castle, Royal Collection, 12778 *recto*; red chalk, 219 × 323 mm; Windsor photo (reproduced with the kind permission of H.M. Queen Elizabeth II).

45. The Dream.—Mentioned by Vasari (*Life of M. A. Raimondi*), this drawing, like the preceding one, presents problems of both authorship and subject. The most suitable interpretation remains the one suggested by Hieronymus Tetius in the seventeenth century (Tolnay). Tetius saw in the youth who, awakened by the trumpet, arises supporting himself on the globe an allegory of the human mind reawakening to virtue from the sleep of sin. The representation of the deadly sins in a circle around the main figure and the masks, symbols of the deceptive appearance of earthly things, seem to confirm this interpretation.

The drawing enjoyed great fame from the moment of its appearance, and many copies were made of it. The conceptuality of the theme, clearly inspired by Neoplatonism, and the almost didactic care in the illustration of it indicate a date around the period of the drawings for Cavalieri. At the same time the broad chiaroscuro presentation of the nude figure has many affinities with the *Resurrected Christ* (Plate 39), while some of the figures of the sins prefigure motifs which will appear in the drawings for *The Last Judgment* as well as even later ones (drawings for *The Prayer in the Garden*, Oxford, Robinson, 70–2). A definite *terminus ante quem* for the dating of this drawing (Marabottini) is offered by a painting by Battista Franco in the Pitti Palace, entitled *The Battle of Montemurlo* and dated 1537, in which the figure of the youth from our drawing is repeated.

London, collection of Count Antoine Seilern (formerly Weimar, collection of the Grand Duke); black chalk, 396 × 278 mm; Bell photo (reproduced with the kind consent of the owner).

46. Study of a Head. Perhaps one of these "stupendous sheets . . . of divine heads" (Vasari) which Michelangelo drew for his friend Cavalieri. The model has been so idealized that it is no longer possible to determine the sex. This study was used for the features of a Madonna in the work of a pupil (Berenson, 1694). The head suggests to me, instead, a male model. The head covering seems to be, rather than a female hair style (Popham-Wilde), the hide of a wild animal.

Perhaps this is the image of a god or a young hero. The face, absorbed in the solitude of meditation, is powerfully thought-provoking.

Windsor Castle, Royal Collection, 12764 *recto*; black chalk, 212 × 142 mm; Windsor photo (reproduced with the kind permission of H.M. Queen Elizabeth II).

47-51. Preparatory Drawings for The Last Judgment.—When Michelangelo left Florence for Rome for the last time in September 1534, Clement VII had already commissioned him to decorate the wall behind the altar in the Sistine Chapel. The Pope died two days after the arrival of the artist, but the commission was renewed by his successor Paul III Farnese. The scaffolding was erected in April 1535. About a year later the preparation of the wall for the fresco was completed and Michelangelo readied himself to begin work on his second great project in the Chapel. As had been the case for the frescoes of the ceiling, almost thirty years earlier, *The Last Judgment* was unveiled on the eve of All Saints' Day, October 31, 1541. Although by now in his sixties, the artist had once again completed the tremendous task without help. The fresco measures about 17 by 13 meters.

47-49. The number of drawings which deal with the total composition of *The Last Judgment* is very small. Among these, however, the three drawings which we illustrate allow us to follow a few successive moments of Michelangelo's plan in the development of the final solution.

In the Bayonne drawing (Plate 47) the figures of the Apostles and the Saints are arranged in an almost complete circle around Christ the Judge, dividing the fresco into two parts—Empyrean above, the crowd of the resurrected below—reflecting a long iconographic tradition.

The relaxing pause that was to come from this arrangement is reflected by a rhythmical balance in the placement of the figures and in their poses which suggests the influence of Raphael (Berenson). The drawing, which in the figure of Christ follows the motif of Zeus in *The Fall of Phaëthon*, must reflect the artist's first ideas for *The Last Judgment* and must date from the end of 1533 or the first months of 1534, that is, from about the same time as the Cavalieri drawings.

The relaxed composition of the Bayonne drawing is superseded by the intensely dramatic one of the Casa Buonarroti sheet (Plate 48). This design is very close to the final one even if at this time Michelangelo still intended to conserve the two lunettes with Patriarchs at the top of the wall (these are replaced in the final version by angels with the symbols of the Passion) and Perugino's fresco of *The Assumption* which was over the altar. There is already in this drawing a continuity of composition, from Christ to the Saints to the Elect to the Damned, which allows the violence of gesture that characterizes every single figure to move uninterrupted through the whole fresco, with a terrifying choral effect.

The articulation of the nudes, which are not yet so gigantic as in the completed fresco, is left, in the Florentine drawing, mainly to the outline. The figures grow larger and more completely articulated in the London drawing (Plate 49) in the group of Saints and Damned on the right. The overdeveloped bodies appear locked in a spasmodic tension suggesting the desperate awareness of the uselessness of their fight.

The difference in time between the first and the two succeeding sheets cannot be more than a few months.

Bayonne, Musée Bonnat, 1217; black chalk, 344 × 290 mm; photo by Archive Photographique des Monuments Historiques.

Florence, Casa Buonarroti, 65 F *recto*; black chalk, 418 × 288 mm; Alinari photo.

London, British Museum, 1895-9-15-518 *recto*; black chalk, 385 × 253 mm; British Museum photo.

50. This is one of the very few "final" drawings for one of the figures of the fresco: the Deacon Lawrence, on the left at the feet of Christ. That this drawing represents a stage envisaging

the final placement of the figure is indicated by the study of the light, which, falling from the left, emphasizes the anatomical articulation of the body while it confers an ardent spirituality upon the head.

Haarlem, Teyler Museum, 13 *recto*; black chalk, 241 × 181 mm; photo by Engel, Haarlem.

51. Figure Study. This figural motif (the head that leans on the right shoulder is barely indicated) seems to be inspired by ancient, especially Hellenistic, statuary (*cf.* the torso of the Rhodian school illustrated in Plate 29 of the *Paradigmata* of Episcopius).

The figure shows exhaustion or lifelessness, and underneath the right armpit are visible the fingers of the hand of a person who offers aid. We recognize this figure grouped with a figure that stands behind it, in the same way as the ancient torso must originally have been composed, in the resurrected man who is lifted bodily in the bottom left of *The Last Judgment* and, with some variations, in the Santa Maria del Fiore and Palestrina *Pietàs*.

The fact that in the *Pietà* of Ubeda—commissioned around 1533 and already under way in 1537—and in the Louvre drawing (No. 716) which is related to it, Sebastiano del Piombo repeats as the Christ this same figure may help to clear up, at least in this case, the nature of the complex relationship between the two artists which lasted about two decades. It is likely that Michelangelo, rather than supplying his friend with drawings executed especially for his paintings, passed on to him studies that he had made from the Antique or in relation to his own compositions, and that these studies were then reinterpreted by the Venetian in his own style.

The drawing of an arm at the bottom of the sheet, a study for one of the angels holding the instruments of the Passion (Barocchi), confirms the dating of this sheet to the first years of the work on *The Last Judgment*.

Florence, Casa Buonarroti, 69 F *recto*; black chalk, 398 × 282 mm; Alinari photo.

52. Cartoon for Three Soldiers from The Crucifixion of St. Peter.—This is a fragment of the cartoon for the fresco on the right wall of the Pauline Chapel. It is made up of nineteen sheets of paper mounted on cloth and shows in the outlines traces of the process of trans-

fer of the design onto the still-fresh plaster of the lower left section of the fresco.

The decoration of the Chapel was commissioned by Paul III Farnese. There are two facing frescoes. *The Conversion of St. Paul* was begun toward the end of 1542 and was finished in 1545. *The Crucifixion of St. Peter* (which was substituted for the originally planned *Consignment of the Keys*—Vasari, 1550 ed.) was begun in March 1546 and was still unfinished in October 1549.

Necessarily of the same dimensions as the fresco, the cartoon exhibits a diffused chiaroscuro superimposed upon the anatomical structure which reduces the energy of the modeling. This development toward a heavier, less articulated treatment of the body is recognizable in the frescoes and reaches its most complete expression in *The Crucifixion of St. Peter*.

The first notice of the cartoon appears in an inventory taken in 1600 of the objects left by Fulvio Orsini to Cardinal Odoardo Farnese.

A large part of the right leg of the soldier who holds the lance comes from a later period. The original sheet has in fact been replaced, apparently because it had deteriorated. A large lacuna in the shoulder and the arm of the same soldier has been repaired with a sheet of white paper.

Naples, Galleria Nazionale di Capodimonte; black chalk, 2.63 × 1.56 m; Anderson photo.

53. The theme of the Madonna and Child reappears once again in this drawing, this time with a tragic intensity that parallels the mood of the Pauline frescoes.

The same frozen monumentality of the group suggests a physical inertia that results from the exaggerated weightiness of the forms. This is opposed by the intensity of the expression on the Madonna's face, and a desperate conflict between the two elements is produced. The date of this drawing, which has been often discussed and is very problematic, can perhaps be pinned down by relating it to a painting by Sofonisba Anguissola. In the *Self-Portrait*, formerly in the Stirling Collection, the young Cremona paintress sits in front of an easel on which rests a painting of the Madonna and Child that clearly reproduces the composition of our drawing. Judging by the apparent age of the young lady, about fifteen or sixteen, the *Self-Portrait* should be dated between 1546 and 1548, a dating which conforms well with the style of Michelangelo's drawing. The student–teacher relationship of Sofonisba and Michelangelo is documented by letters of the girl's father (Tolnay) and by a letter of Cavalieri's of 1562.

At some time in the past the background of the drawing was covered by gold, altering, in part, the contour of the group.

Windsor Castle, Royal Collection, 12772 *recto*; black chalk, 225 × 194 mm; Windsor photo (reproduced with the kind permission of H.M. Queen Elizabeth II).

54. Christ Expels the Money-Changers from the Temple.—This composition, from which a painting was made by Marcello Venusti (now in the National Gallery in London), was preceded by two other studies of the same theme. All are now in the British Museum. The rhythmical cadence of the gestures, the wide proportions of the figures and the more summary anatomical definition contrasted with the strengthened outline indicate a date near the period of the last work in the Pauline Chapel.

Venusti worked in close contact with Michelangelo, especially during the last decade or so of the master's life, translating many of his designs into paintings. It is to him that we owe the finest extant copy of *The Last Judgment* (Naples, Galleria di Capodimonte), executed for Cardinal Alessandro Farnese.

London, British Museum, 1860-6-16-2/3 *recto* (the drawing is composed of six irregular sheets); black chalk, 178 × 372 mm; Alinari photo.

55. Epiphany.—This and the cartoon in Naples (Plate 52) are the only cartoons by Michelangelo which have been preserved. The master's cartoons were much fought over by his pupils and admirers, so that, when they were not hopelessly damaged by the transfer of the design onto the wall or burnt by the artist, they were dispersed and destroyed. The present cartoon was mentioned in the notary's inventory (February 19, 1564) of the works found in the house of Macel de' Corvi on the day following the death of Michelangelo. It is probably this cartoon which Ascanio Condivi copied in a panel painting now in the Casa Buonarroti (Vasari).

The *Epiphany*, as the cartoon is referred to in the document of April 21, 1564, shows the same figure type as the Pauline frescoes. The composition repeats, on a simplified scale, the scheme of those frescoes. It is composed of a triangular prism whose edge projects out toward the viewer. It shows a desire to involve the spectator in an immediate and direct way in the scene which is represented.

A date around 1550 for the cartoon is indicated also by the notices concerning Condivi's Roman sojourn.

London, British Museum, 1895-9-15-518; black chalk and charcoal, 2.327 × 1.656 m; British Museum photo.

56. The Virgin of the Annunciation.—Vasari mentions two *Annunciations* which Venusti "colored" from Michelangelo's drawings. The first, which is lost but known through copies, was for the Cesi Chapel in Santa Maria della Pace. The second was done for the Church of San Giovanni in Laterano (now in the sacristy).

The figure in the London drawing does not exactly correspond to the Virgin in either the first or the second composition, but, because she is seated and turns with accentuated torsion to her left, she seems more to foreshadow the Virgin of the Cesi altarpiece. The refurbishment of the Cesi Chapel took place toward the middle of the century (Wilde) and the drawing must date from that period. The increased sketchiness of the anatomical articulation and the diffusion of shadow that reduces the overwhelming plasticity of the figure point to a moment not far from the last activity in the Pauline Chapel.

London, British Museum, 1900-6-11-1 *recto*; black chalk, 348 × 224 mm; Alinari photo.

57. Sketches for a Pietà.—Michelangelo returned to the theme of the dead Christ (he had treated it once before in one of the drawings for Vittoria Colonna) insistently during the period around 1550, half a century after the Vatican *Pietà*. Christ is no longer stretched out on the lap of the Virgin as in that early *Pietà*. Instead, in the three marble *Pietàs* of the last decade and a half of the artist's life, the Santa Maria del Fiore, the Palestrina and the Rondanini *Pietàs*, which the artist worked on until the eve of his death, the extenuated body is held up to the view of the faithful by Joseph

29

of Arimathea or the Virgin. The inspiration for this pose could have been, as we have noted (Plate 51), Hellenistic sculpture, but the final solution is anti-classical and actually anti-Renaissance in feeling. There is a progressive and most decided whittling away of the plasticity of the figure, to the point where it becomes an image of purely spiritual value.

Stages from this last phase of the art of Michelangelo are documented in the figures sketched out on this sheet in a series filled with intense drama.

Oxford, Ashmolean Museum, Robinson 70(1); black chalk, 108 × 281 mm; Ashmolean Museum photo.

58 & 59. The Crucifixion. Treatments of the subject of the crucified Christ recur, separated sometimes by many years, throughout Michelangelo's long career, from the wooden *Christ* of his youth in Santo Spirito in Florence, to the "live" Christ on the Cross (Condivi) inspired by the intense piety of Vittoria Colonna about 1540, and finally to the group of drawings for a *Crucifixion* datable to the fifties, of which these drawings in Oxford and London are part.

Next to the dead Christ on the Cross appear either the Virgin and St. John (Plate 59), following the traditional iconography, or the centurion and Longinus (Plate 58—Tolnay is responsible for this stimulating identification). In both cases the significance which the figures assume in the context of Michelangelo's composition is unusual. In the Oxford drawing, the last act of the tragedy has barely been completed. A trace of it is to be seen in Christ's last breath, still inflating the torso of the figure. The sudden revelation ("and there was a darkness over all the earth . . . And the sun was darkened . . . ," Luke 23: 44–45) falls with terrifying force upon the two soldiers,

elevated into symbols of the guilt of all humanity. The artist searches for escape from this desperate condition in the act of humility and love which locks the Virgin and St. John to the foot of the cross. The Mother, whose almost weightless body is suggested by countless strokes of a light line, is reunited with Christ, who is represented as an image of more than human peace and beauty, in which soft shadows surround and thin the youthful limbs. This is almost an act of renunciation by the artist of his own powerfully sculptural ideal. At the same time it is a lofty message of faith. The Oxford drawing, because it is closer to the plastic character of the Pauline frescoes, must predate the London drawing by a few years.

Oxford, Ashmolean Museum, Robinson 72 *recto*; black chalk, 278 × 234 mm; Ashmolean Museum photo.

London, British Museum, 1895-9-15-510; black chalk, 412 × 279 mm; British Museum photo.

60. Madonna and Child.—This drawing is generally considered to be one of the last drawings of Michelangelo, if not the last, and for more than one reason is associated with the Virgin in the *Crucifixion* in London (Plate 59). Here, too, the physical presence of the figure seems to exist only as a function of the timorous expression of love which ties the Mother to the Child. This is a pure image, illuminated from within, where the succession of waving and broken chalk lines, rather than suggesting the faltering hand of an old man, confirms the great capacity of the artist to express himself always with completeness in the most accomplished and unequivocal way.

London, British Museum, 1859-6-25-562; black chalk, 266 × 117 mm; British Museum photo.

1 Figure study after Giotto's *Apotheosis of St. John the Baptist*

2 Figure study after Masaccio's *Sagra of the Carmine*

3 Five studies

4 Study for a *Mercury* (?)

5 Madonna and Child with St. Anne

6 Sketch for a bronze *David*

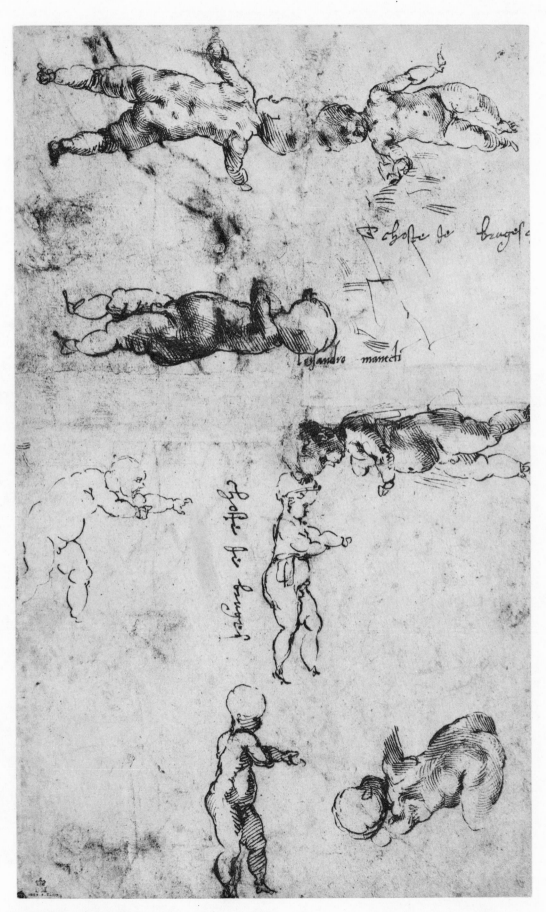

7 Studies of cherubs

8 Various studies

9 Study for *The Battle of Cascina*: Cavalry battle

10 Study for *The Battle of Cascina*: Young male nude

11 Study for *The Battle of Cascina*: Studies of figures and *The Madonna of Bruges*

12 Study for *The Battle of Cascina*: Studies of figures

13 Study for *The Battle of Cascina*: Nude

14 Study for *The Battle of Cascina*: Nude

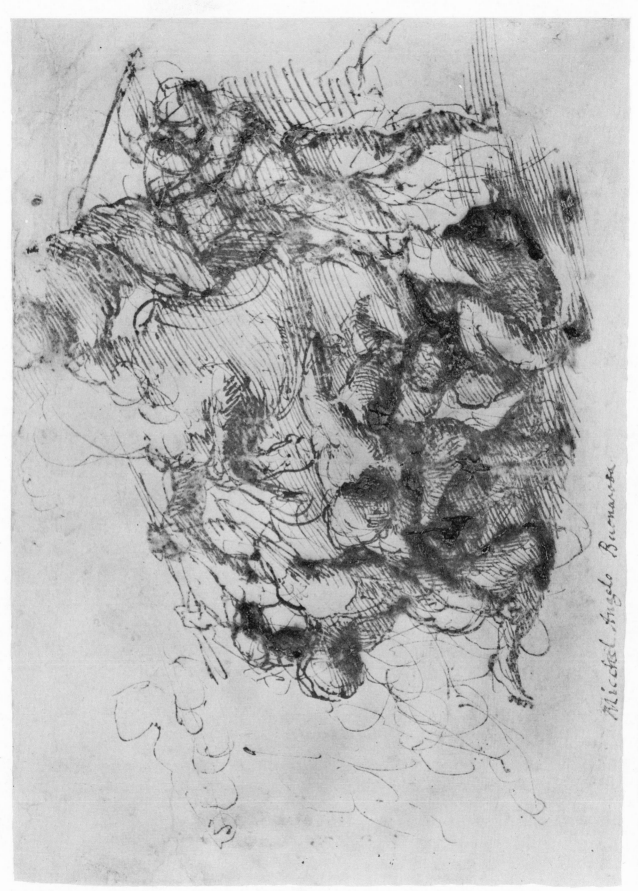

15 Study for *The Battle of Cascina*: Skirmish between cavalry and foot soldiers

16 Study of a nude

17 Madonna and Child with St. Anne

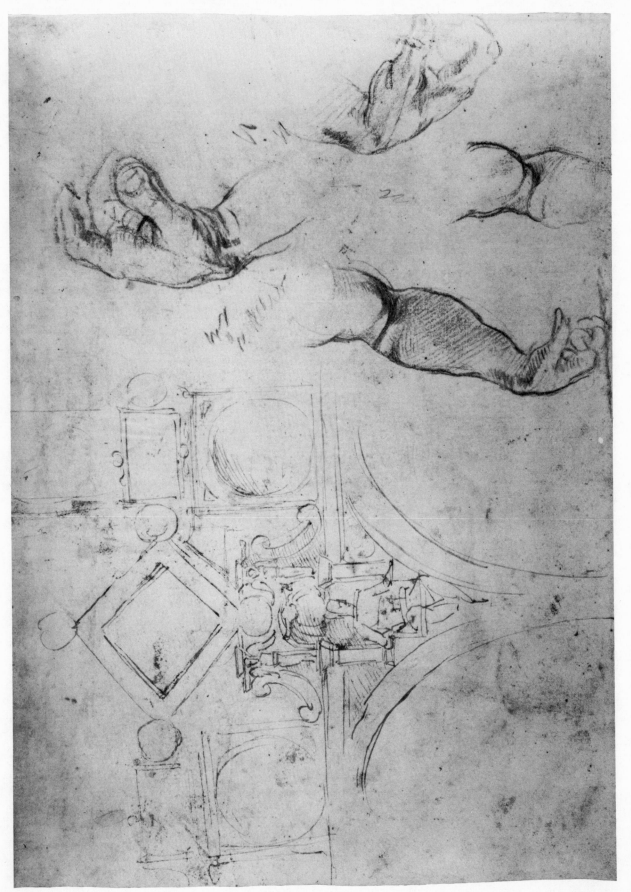

18 Study for the Sistine ceiling: Architectural project with Apostles

19 Study for the Sistine ceiling: Adam in *The Expulsion from Paradise*

20 Study for the Sistine ceiling: Head of an old man

21 Study for the Sistine ceiling: Head of a young man

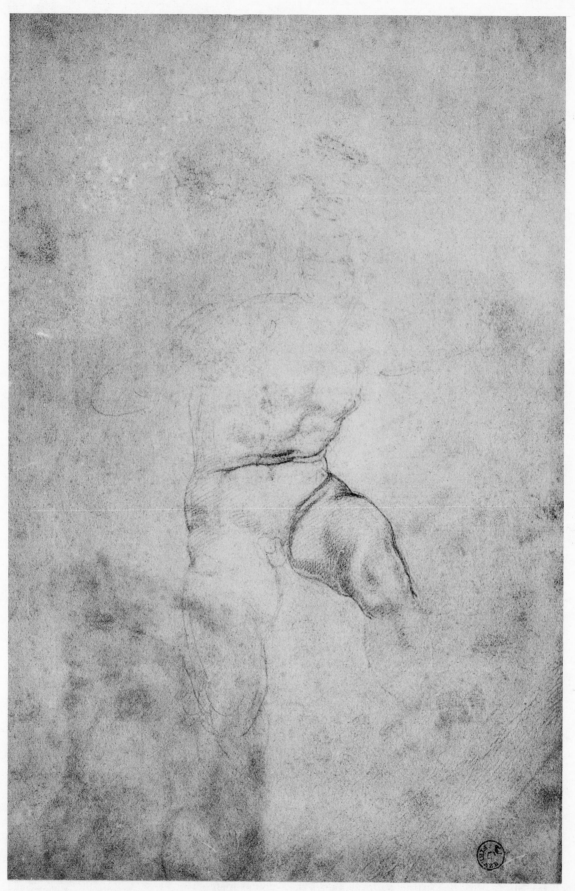

22 Study for the Sistine ceiling: Nude

23 Study for the Sistine ceiling: Head

24 Study for the Sistine ceiling: The Libyan Sibyl

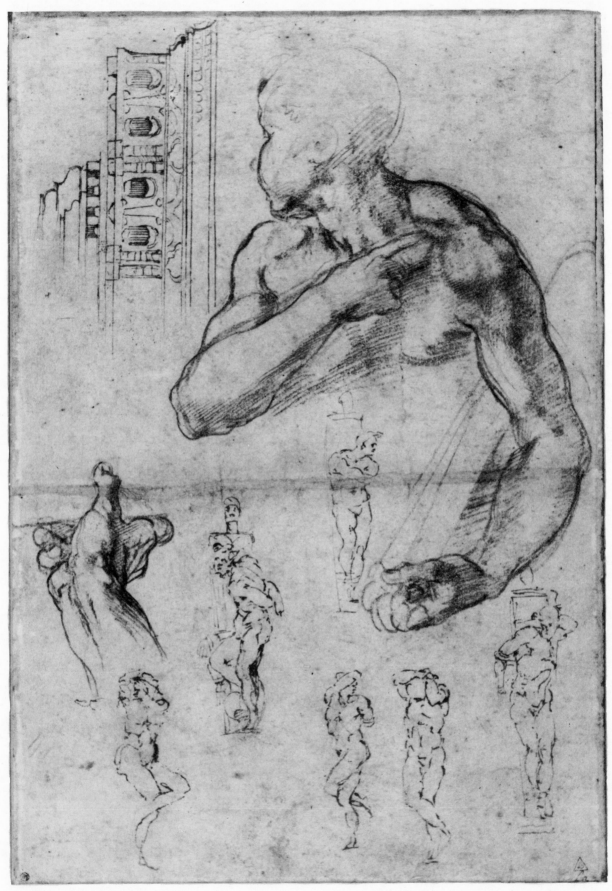

25 Study for the Sistine ceiling: *Genietto*

26 Study for a Prophet (?)

27 Study of a female head

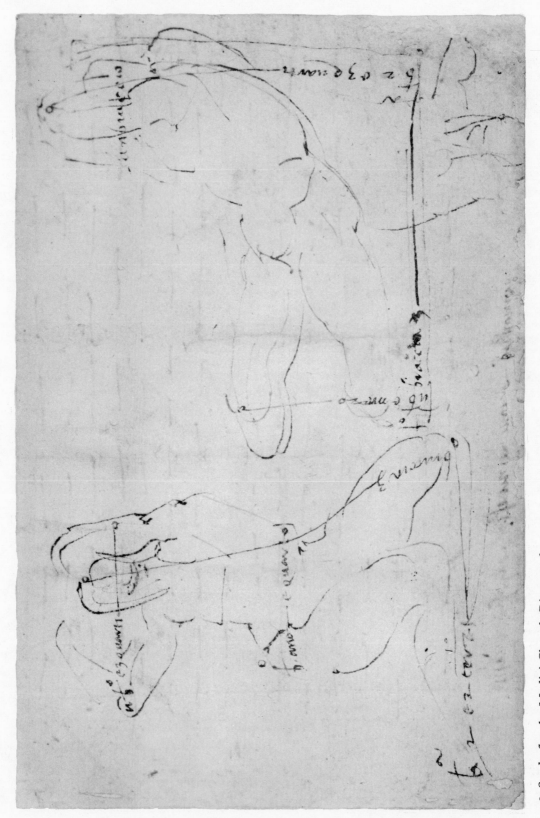

28 Study for the Medici Chapel: River god

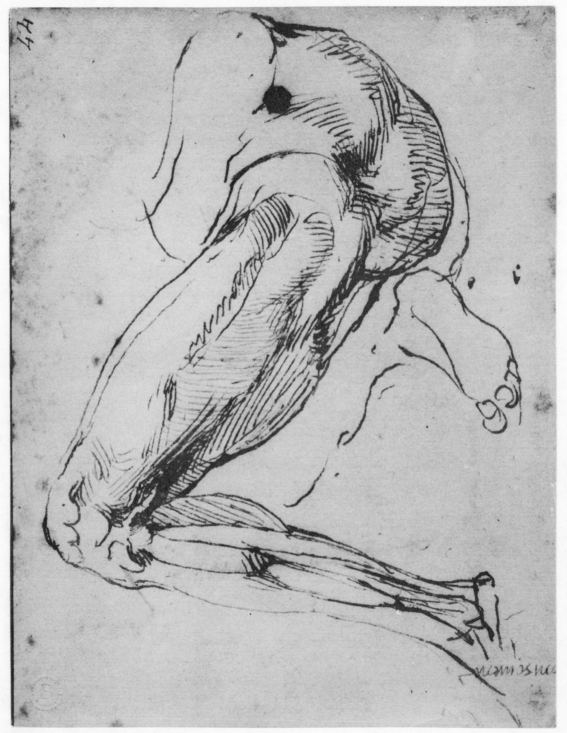

29 Study for the Medici Chapel: Anatomical study

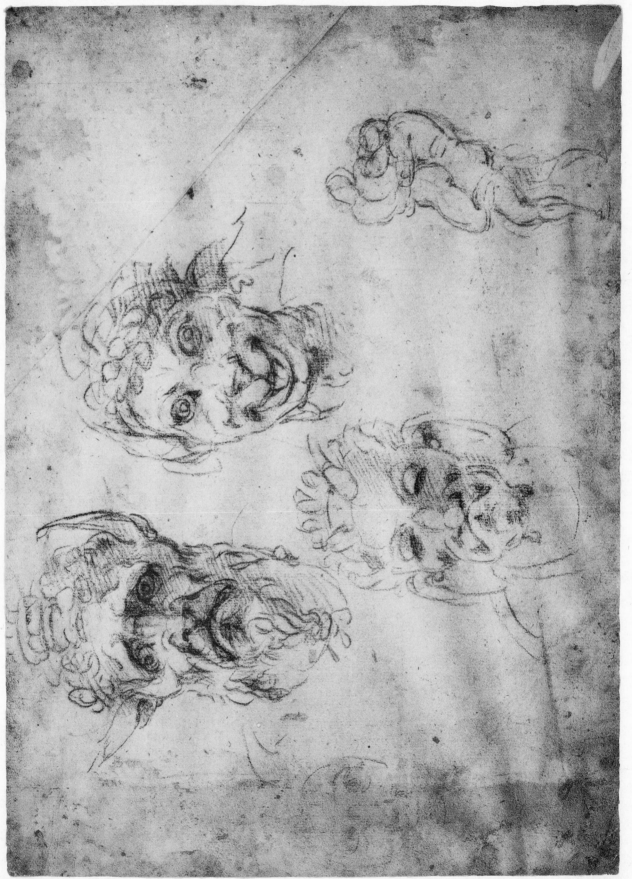

30 Study for the Medici Chapel: Grotesque heads

31 Study for the Medici Chapel: Monstrous animal

32 Study for a *Madonna and Child*

33 Study for a *Holy Family*

34 Head of a young man

35 Head of a young woman

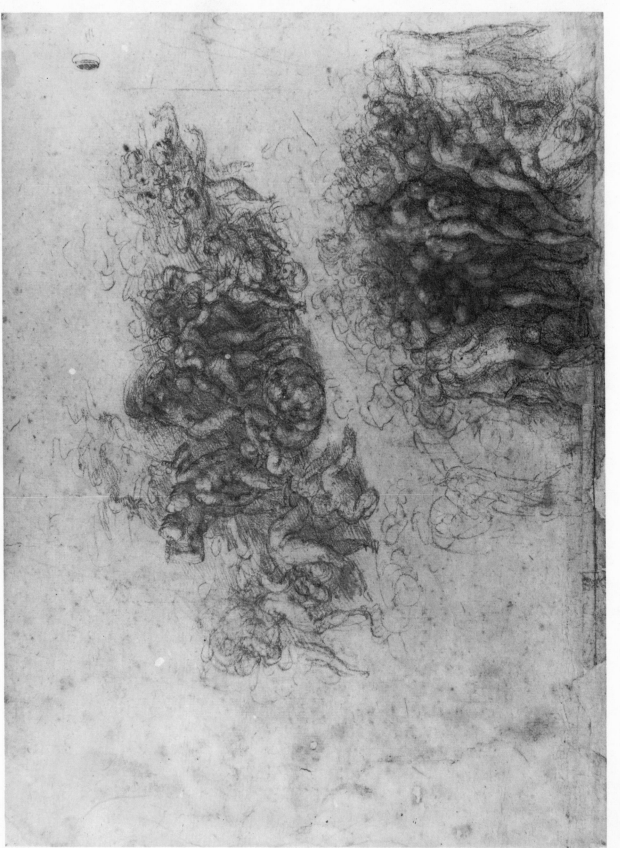

36 Study for an *Adoration of the Bronze Serpent*

37 Study for a *Resurrection*

38 Study for a *Resurrection*

39 Study for a *Resurrected Christ*

40 Figure study

41 Sacrifice of Isaac

42 Tityus

43 Fall of Phaëthon

44 The Archers

45 The Dream

46 Study of a head

47 Study for *The Last Judgment*: Compositional study

48 Study for *The Last Judgment*: Compositional study

49 Study for *The Last Judgment*: Compositional study

50 Study for *The Last Judgment*: The Deacon Lawrence

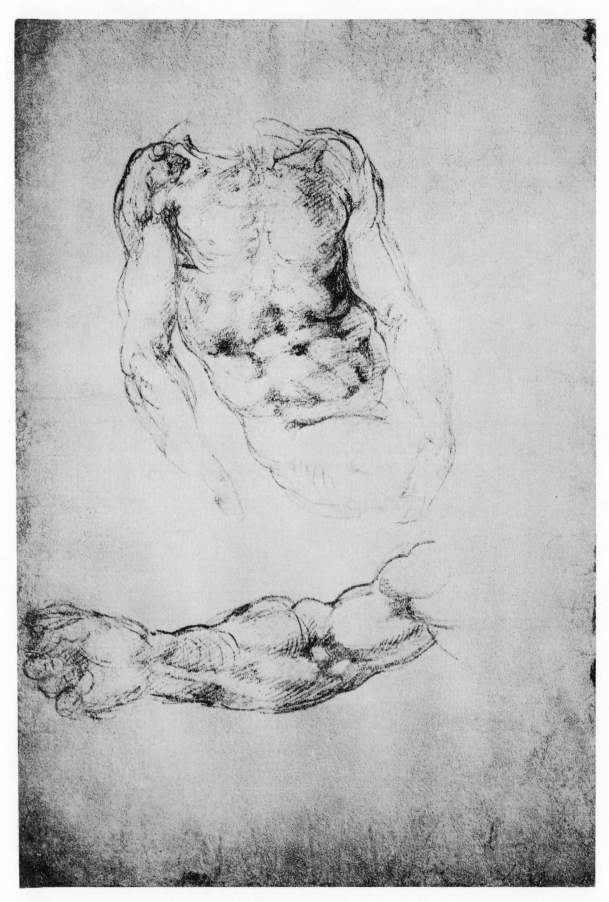

51 Study for *The Last Judgment*: Figure study

52 Cartoon for three soldiers from *The Crucifixion of St. Peter*

53 Madonna and Child

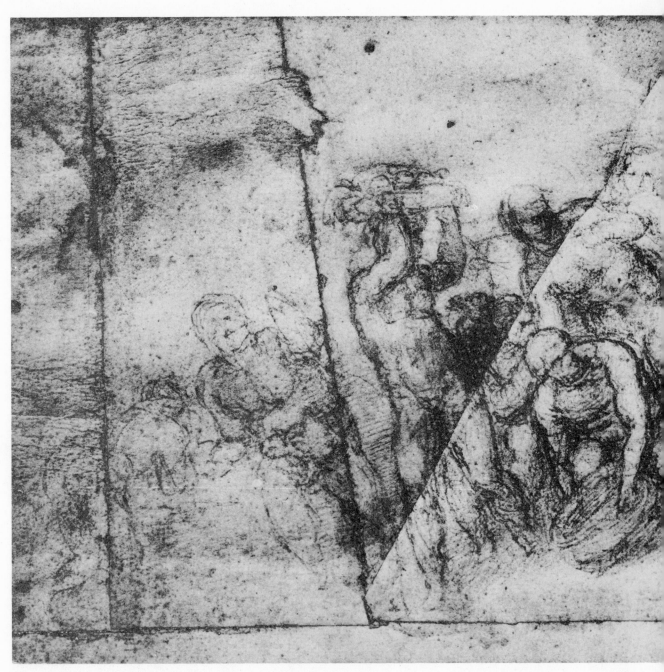

54 Christ expels the money-changers from the Temple

55 Epiphany

56 The Virgin of the Annunciation

57 Sketches for a *Pietà*

58 The Crucifixion

59 The Crucifixion

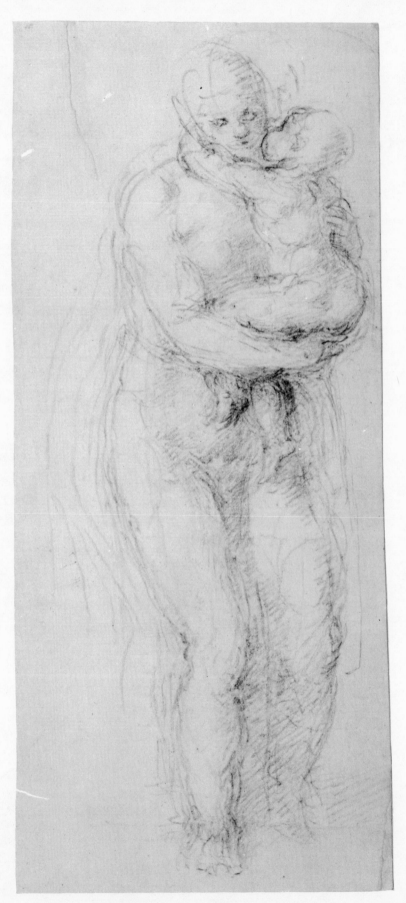

60 Madonna and Child